WOMEN LIKE ME

Breaking Through The Silence

JULIE FAIRHURST

Contents

Introduction

JULIE FAIRHURST

"But silence is not a natural environment for stories.
They need words. Without them they grow pale, sicken, and
die. And then they haunt you."
— Diane Setterfield

The Authors in volume four of Women Like Me – Breaking Through the Silence are powerful women. They know the damage that keeping secrets and not speaking up for yourself can do overtime. Every time a woman keeps silent, it teaches the next generation of women that we still need to stay silent, to remain quiet.

It's not healthy to keep secrets, even small ones. There can be a lot of anxiety and stress, which can lead to depression. You hold it in your mind and body. It's always in the back of your mind. When you release it through your voice or writing, you can let go and not be held down by it.

Not speaking up is also being silent. Whether you are not speaking up for yourself or a loved one, you will be feeling the same stresses and anxiety in your mind and body. Not speaking when you know you need to will leave you feeling frustrated and even helpless. And none of us are helpless!

Examine your childhood. It was here where you would have learned to communicate. What was happening in your home? Did you try to speak up and were shut down? Were you told to "keep quiet" about a situation that had or was happening to you or someone you loved? Were you told you were not telling the truth? How were you shut down?

Some of us would have been respected and praised for speaking up. Unfortunately, for many women, it would have been the opposite. When you can understand how the communication was in your home, you will start to understand why you communicate the way you do. And you can't fix something until you know it's broken. This is why you want to think back about your family's communication style.

Most women experience troubles at some point in their lives. Those troubles can leave feelings of being alone. Life can be messy, and not everything is going to go our way, and over time our situations can seem impossible.

If you want to find inner peace, you must release the secrets you have been holding and learn to speak up for yourself and others. When you don't speak up, you may give the impression that you are okay with what people say to you or to those you love.

I believe this. We teach people how to treat us! When we are quiet, it says it is okay to treat me the way you are or speak to me in that manner. Your silence may be viewed as acceptance.

Psycholgytoday.com says that people are afraid to speak up for themselves. The biggest reason for this is fear of rejection or the judgment of others. These two reasons hold so many of us back from living our best lives.

The benefits of speaking up and no longer being silent will allow you to become more confident. And when you have confidence, you'll naturally show the other women in your life that it's okay to speak up. You will inspire others in your world to do the same and voice their opinions, release their secrets, and feel safe. You can change someone's entire life through your example.

In this book, you are going to discover eleven women who decided not to hide anymore, to speak up for themselves, and to speak up for their loved ones.

Being an advocate for senior's trying to navigate through the medical system. They are standing up for themselves and others who have disabilities and fighting for help — pushing through the feelings of shame to tell stories of addiction and how they overcame — speaking up about the injustice of our legal system and racism. And the courage to tell a story about losing love and finding it again.

These are courageous women. They are Women Like Me, and they will no longer be silent.

ONE

GREEN BUTTERFLY

ON A WING AND A PRAYER

"Our wounds are often the openings to the best and most
beautiful part of us."
David Richo

Good day. The fact that you are here, reading this, makes me suspect you are open and willing or searching to connect through your heart. I hope my story can give you or a loved one a sense of hope and to know you are not alone.

Let me start by saying that when I was in college shaking my booty on the bar at Stages Nightclub and when I was having the time of my life kickin up my heels to "Any Man of Mine" at the local saloon, it never once crossed my mind that one of my favorite things to do would turn my future life completely upside down, inside out and twist it all to shit...

It all started back on January 29th, 1972, when all 5 lbs and 13 oz of Shannon Rose (me) arrived on this spectacular planet filled with lots of color, lots of love, and lots of fear.

Everyone said I was the cutest baby with the biggest, brightest brown eyes. My anxious and empathic mom also said I had a terrorizing scream that would wake the neighbors. Back about 50 years ago, having an intolerance to milk and wheat was not on the radar as a cause for a baby's high-pitched shrieking cry.

From that point on, for several years, my mom was constantly running me to the hospital with ear infections, tonsillitis, and "rolling on the floor" stomach pain. I spent several nights in the hospital recovering from ear, tonsil, and sinus surgeries in those early years. I still remember, to this day, my fear of that very painful "green butterfly" IV needle going into my hand before surgery. It is beyond me why they would call a needle a "butterfly". It was very scary for five-year-old me when the nurses had to pin me down every time that enormous X-ray machine would come down upon me. I remember wondering if my mom was going to come back for me. With the work that I have done, I understand now that was the feeling of abandonment. Being hospitalized can be traumatizing for a child.

I have since learned that childhood trauma can appear in many forms, and it's not about what happens to the child but what happens inside of them. Children are not traumatized because they are hurt but because they are alone in their hurt.

Being an empath myself, even though mom did her best to hide her fear, I knew she was run ragged, caring, and worrying about me. I felt like a burden. It wasn't just me. She was a mom to my three brothers too. Yep, there were more kiddies two years after I was born. I had to move over to fit in brother

#1, and boy oh boy, I could write a chapter on him and me alone, then 11 months after that brother #2, and then two years after that brother #3.

Mom and Dad sure had their hands full with us and more. They are the hardest working people I know with the biggest hearts. They didn't just care for us; our home was the drop-in house for any extended family members or neighbors that needed support, whether it was a meal, a bed, a hitch out of the ditch, fixing a flat, or just a shoulder to cry on. Mom and Dad still to this day, just keep on giving.

Okay, enough about and them back to me because it's all about me, haha.

Being the only girl with three brothers, I quickly picked up the "tomboy" label. My favorite Christmas gift as a kid was "Stretch Armstrong" which was a bodybuilder male doll, and you could pull and stretch him. It was a disappointing day when he leaked out all over the floor.

A few of my favorite and memorable pastimes were tromping through the pond catching frogs with the boys, shoveling shit and feeding the cows with grandpa Ted up at the barn, driving our dirt bike through big mud holes, and pulling each other on the toboggan behind the skidoo. The boys and I pretty much lived outside from sunrise to sundown and loved every minute of it.

Omg, I could tell you so many stories, lots of great stories, and some that affected me negatively. When I was seven years old, I was on the back of the snowmobile behind the driver, who decided to get off to check on something. I thought I could drive this thing and drove it full speed towards a parked bus, and adding to that terror as our parents watched, there was a car hood filled with kids attached to the back. The car hood was my dad's very clever Redneck version of a toboggan.

Omg, I will never forget that day. I can remember my mom's cousin, who was on the hood, thank god, had to push all the kids off to save their lives. I remember his eyebrows full of snow, and I saw the terror in his eyes. Yes, you guessed it, we hit the bus. The dear Lord was with us because somehow I just turned enough in the nick of time that the windshield and steering just grazed it, but the car hood did go underneath. I ended up with an injured hand and the rest were covered in snow and pounding hearts. Even though no one was physically injured, it was one of those near tragedies that had post-traumatic effects. This is one of the many experiences as a child that left me believing I was a bad girl for causing all this trouble.

When I was eight, grandpa got off the tractor to open the gate, well you know me, yep I once again did it, not only was I driving the tractor out of control, I flattened a fence heading towards grandpa, he must have had Angels with him that day because he literally flew up onto that moving tractor to save himself and me. God Bless him, being a parent now, I understand entirely the terror on his face that day.

These experiences and others played over and over and over in my head. I think that is when the anxiety and panic set into my body and mind.

Without a doubt, my grandpa Ted was my favorite person in the whole wide world. When I was with him, I didn't feel fearful. I felt safe and important. I loved spending time with him and grandma. The Friday night Tommy Hunter Show and Hee

Haw were not my favorite shows, but I didn't care because I was with them. I was their "Precious Lub " the pet name they gave me, which always made me feel special. Gramps would always say, "I love you a whole big lot," and to this day, I still write that in my loved one's birthday cards in honor of him and due to the depth of love I feel for them.

During sleepovers at gram and gramps, one of my favorite jobs was to help take care of my grandma's mom "Nana" who lived with them. She was a stroke survivor in a wheelchair and needed help going to the bathroom, eating, taking her pills, and drinking. I loved that little caregiver role; it was meaningful, and I had a purpose.

There was one hitch about staying with grandma: we had to pray, a lot! I call it the marathon of praying. It felt like hours; first, we would say the rosary, then read the milk bag full of prayer cards, next we would God Bless every single person we knew and finish it off with "Now I lay me down to sleep...". I am eternally grateful for those memories now and still pray every day and still rely on St. Anthony every time we need to find something we lost. Thank you, St. Anthony, for helping us find our keys, wallets, cell phones, and more.

Throughout the years, I endured more pain, digestive issues, and many years of hating myself and God for being so fat. It was humiliating wearing a size 20 quilt to grade 9 and occupying the nickname "Sherm" for Sherman Tank. I was told that smoking would help you lose weight, so I took that up right away, and honestly, it did help with shedding some pounds and also led to torture down the road trying to quit.

In my early twenties, as my anxiety, drinking, and smoking progressed, my mom ran me into the hospital again. About five years after that, I was finally diagnosed with Crohns disease and medicated for anxiety. That is another long road of healing that I will save for the next book.

On May 31st, 1997, at age 25, I got married to the love of my life. My health had been up and down, so we were cautious about when to have a baby. To our surprise, I was pregnant sooner than expected. My husband and I were so excited also fearful that I might have a Crohns flare-up. However, the doctors said it was safe to stay on steroids, and the pregnancy was great, and our little bug was small but healthy and strong.

We were all so happy, surprised, and extremely thrilled to have the first girl in our family. She was #6 in the lineup of the first five boy cousins born ahead of her. Then, a couple more years later, her very energetic and beat to his own drum brother was born. My poor little monkey, I'm sure, felt much distress during my pregnancy with him. At that time, the kids' dad and I were having marital troubles.

When the kids were three and five, we separated. It was a very confusing time for the kids. Of course, they didn't understand why. It was a very challenging and heartbreaking time for all of us.

Growing up in a strict Irish Catholic home, you get married in the church, "till death due us part". I carried much shame having a failed marriage. Being Catholic was a huge part of our life. The boys and I attended a Catholic school, and we went to church every weekend. We even went those weekends in our late teens and early twenties hungover; mom forcefully invited us and any of our friends who stayed from the party the night before. Oh, dear God, I am sure our pew reeked of booze, but we were there, God willing. I continued going to church until that day, that day you will hear about later. Haha, here I go again, getting off-topic. Back to life after separation...

Life painfully moved on, and the emotional rollercoaster ride continues as a single mom. And you single moms understand the toll it takes working full time, coaching soccer, trying to please everyone, giving all you've got to fix everyone and everything around you. You completely lose yourself in the process. **Ahha, but there is a solution for that. DRINK.** So, I turned to and leaned on what became the loves of my life, beer and wine.

It sure took the edge off and gave me that ease and comfort that I needed at the end of each stressful day and during those lonely weekends. BUT... then it turned on me, it wasn't just the end of the day or on weekends anymore, I was now drinking every day, day and night. I was missing work, losing friends, and hurting the most precious people in my life. My two beautiful children and I hated myself for it. I didn't understand that I was a sick woman. I thought I was a terrible person, a horrible mother.

However, through all of that, I managed with help from other loved ones to raise two incredible now adult children who are a product of a mom recovering from alcoholism, a broken belief system, anxiety, and in recovery from a severe autoimmune disorder. I know to the average joe, this sounds like a bit of a "Shit Show," and no pun intended, well maybe pun intended since I do have that "do do" type autoimmune disorder... to tell the truth, it sure was a Shit Show. Stay tuned. It does get better, haha.

It was September 19th, 2013. I had three options in my head. I was going to slice my wrists, go to the Psych Ward, or do the last thing I wanted to do quit drinking. I already tried to cut back a thousand times and a hundred different ways. I couldn't do it. I literally crawled out of bed that morning, my body saturated with booze and unable to drive to work again. I had finally hit my intensely painful emotional, physical and spiritual rock bottom. I couldn't do it anymore. I couldn't hurt the most precious people in the world anymore, and I didn't have anything left in me. I did the hardest thing in the world because, you know, "I don't need any man to take out my garbage."

I ASKED FOR HELP. I sobbed and sobbed, heading to my moms, and spilled all of it to her. Mom is not a stranger to the disease of alcoholism since it's in our family's blood. She cared for and helped me through the detoxing process.

That same night terrified and shaking like a leaf, I went to my first 12 Step meeting. The people there talked about their healing, they told their story, and it was my story. They explained all the same feelings, the darkness, pain, guilt, shame, and remorse. I was finally able to surrender, and I finally let these amazing happy sober people help me.

I'm not going to lie; being in recovery the first year was like being turned inside out. I wanted to hide in my skin away from the world, and at the same time, I also wanted to jump out of my skin because I couldn't stand being in it. During this intense change and transformation, I was carried, led, and loved by others who had already been through it all. They loved me until I learned to love myself.

They taught me to set healthy boundaries. You see, when I was drinking, I spent most of my time with my family, and most of them drank, so it was extremely difficult and very lonely stepping away from the ones I loved the most, but it was more lonely being with them and not drinking. It was like wearing an itchy sweater all the time, feeling restless and irritable all the time. For me to get relief, I had to do the work. To survive and find happiness, I had to clean up and brighten up my insides. So, I started this gruelling yet brilliant process...

At 4½ months sober, I picked up a drink because I couldn't get my son to church and was fearful to face my parents. I thought I was a terrible mom, so I picked up a drink, but I stopped for the first time in my life. I can't really explain it; it all just didn't feel right. You see, I had learned enough during those few months of healing to know that I needed to care for myself, so I did something that is almost forbidden for women in my family I went for a nap for the first time in my life. I had to shut my brain off, and to my surprise, it actually worked. It helped cut the anxiety, and all the other feelings that went along with this terrible discomfort, almost like the booze did. And now I don't give two shits what others think about me napping. That nap that day might have just saved my life.

That is the day, at 41 years old, I realized my religious belief system was not serving me any longer. It was causing turmoil inside of me. It was scary and completely against my conditioning, but I let go of this belief system I was entrenched in. I pulled my children from their altar serving positions and detached from the church.

That day was really the first day that I began my spiritual healing journey. I was building a new relationship with my great universal spirit. It was completely different from the religious one I grew up with, and it was part of me, a great spiritual connection filled with loving energy, no judgment, and a heart connection to others.

It was no longer the guy in the sky with a beard. I can feel this peace, joy, and gratitude everywhere. I see and experience tiny hummingbirds that come in with kisses. I hear the wind in the trees and the loving words of encouragement that come through others. I gratefully breathe in deeply, inhaling the fresh air that is available to us. I so very much appreciate peace and stillness now, and the many moments I feel gratitude for the simplest things. Gosh, my heart is so full just writing this. I thought I was a bad person for many years when really, I was a sick person with a broken spirit.

Remember earlier when I said it never occurred to me that my life would be turned upside down... as I was shaking a leg at the local bars? Well, here is another one of the most significant lessons I learned during this life changing time.

This one day, I was cutting carrots, and my kids were sitting at the counter across from me. I was having a really tough day during this transformation, and I wasn't able to communicate with the kids, and I couldn't stop crying. I called my spiritual mentor, and she said, "Miss Shannon, you are giving your children the best "GIFT" you can give them." I was like, "WTF." She said, "they saw you vomit on yourself, sick with your disease, they saw you crying, unable to communicate and, they are watching you transform into the shining light that you are. They know that they too can be human, that it's ok to cry, be sick, reach out for help and transform too." The funny thing, and not so funny, is that that exact thing happened with my daughter. She has had to reach out for help. She also attended support meetings, talked with an addiction counselor, and is a shining thriving Electrical Apprentice today.

My son is in the midst of his addiction was able to reach out to me because I am sober and healthy to support him. As a matter of fact, I rushed home this morning to be with him in his sick, broken state. Tonight me, my brother, partner, and other friends are taking him to our 12 Step meeting. I can walk with my son. I have the right contacts, and I have an open heart, arms, and understanding to carry him at this time. This being said, it's now a couple of days after, and having an open conversation with my son, he said he wants more for his life. He heard in that meeting that he is not alone and there is much hope for his future. (Thank you, dearest great spirit for this healing.)

When I made my amends to my son, it was a conversation about how not everyone in our family liked that I was sober. He said, "Mom, I am so happy you are sober, I never want you to drink again". He loved that we could go for ice cream on a Saturday night and that he could count on me to take him to the hospital when he had a stomach ache or anxiety attack. The interesting thing is that his stomach pains stopped soon after I quit drinking. My kids shared with me after that they were terrified that I would hurt or kill myself and didn't want to lose their mom.

Now I am giving back in so many ways. I am helping other women heal, find peace, find their voice, speak their truth and live authentically.

My life is richer, my spiritual connection is deepening, my relationships are heart-connected, and I am more grateful than struggling. Don't get me wrong; it's not all rainbows and butterflies. Some days it's like the "Green Butterfly", It hurts a lot, full of fear, and some days I am all fucked up and fall apart. I am a human being, not perfect, but I am a courageous woman who keeps going. I am content with where I am and very eager to get where I am going.

I went back to school and successfully achieved a Stress and Wellness Consultant Diploma, a Reflexology Certification, and a few other healing certifications. It is in my heart and my being to help others heal. It is very meaningful to see other women like me transform from pain, a broken spirit, to seeing hope in their eyes and rise up into this shining star. AHHH-HHH. Fills my heart.

I need to give thanks to so many. There is no way I could have survived on my own. There are no words for how much appreciation I have for my very supportive and loving mom and dad, my incredible children, all of my many mental and physical therapists. My partner who walks by my side each day and my dearest spiritual fellowship. Thank you, Thank you, Thank you All. I love you a Whole Big Lot.

Please know, dear reader:
You are not alone
It is OK to reach out for help.
You are a human being, a good shit and DEEPLY LOVED
I wish you peace.
I wish you love.
And I wish you much joy.

Shannon Levee

TWO

A SPECIAL VISIT

WHEN YOU ASK FOR A MIRACLE

"The passing of someone we love leaves a hole in our heart that never fills. But warm memories can help keep them close."
Unknown

My life started to ease up when a lime green Luna moth decided to rest on the ceiling of my art shop back in, I think 2014. Unfortunately, I honestly can't remember the exact dates, just as I couldn't tell you the precise year that my daughter Katie committed suicide. I know, right? What I do know is she died on September 19. I only remember because I wrote the date in my prayer book at some point in time. Then two weeks later, I fell in the front yard and badly fractured my ankle. It's surprising; I remember anything at all in the state I was in.

While I was glued to the sofa for weeks, I was able to think. I remember I had a lot of time to reflect - a time to rest and look at my own life. One realization was, I quickly learned who my real friends were. People whom I thought were close were simply passing friends. Hurt, oh yes! I felt lost and hurt from being passively set aside but thank goodness I developed new friends and cemented old friends. I started surrounding myself with positive people.

Friends who cared, whether they knew how or even knew what to say, were the friends who comforted me. Who were there for me! They knitted with me, stopped to chat with me. They painted with me. They enjoyed my company, and I wanted them. They were a lovely distraction while I was struggling with depression. Not many people realized I felt broken losing my child, my child whom I gave birth to. I needed these friends to be with me, and I wanted to be with them.

So as time passed, a lovely surprise happened in my life. It was months later when this happened. A lovely lime green Luna moth visited me. My favorite color! I believe she stayed for two weeks. It was so amazing. I took photos and watched this green moth like it was my very own pet. I felt so many emotions, excitement, sadness, you name it, I felt it all. It was my sign from the Universe that all was going to be all right. I truly believe this was a spiritual experience for me. This lovely creature appeared like a miracle just for me.

I believe in God, the Universe, or whatever you want to pray to, will gift you a sign. Trust that a SIGN will appear to you. I believe this! I BELIEVE GOD will grant you what you want. I will take this a step further. So, I'm Catholic; we believe in Mary, the mother of Jesus, who listens to our prayers and helps guide us. I believe the Blessed Mother Mary, the mother of the baby Jesus, will grant you whatever you desire if you simply ask. I know she will. All you have to do is ask her, and she will receive or ask the Universe, ask the God of the power you believe in.

So a surprising and wonderful thing happened from that day; I would begin to see butterflies every day. Either real butterflies or images. I could be watching TV, and someone would be wearing a butterfly-printed shirt or butterfly art on the wall. Even to this day, I see butterflies all around me. A tote bag, dishware, paintings, tattoos, they are everywhere. I feel seeing these butterflies are signs from Katie letting me know she is always around me. I have so many photos because I would take photos of a butterfly each day with excitement for two to three years. I still do on occasion if it's an unusual butterfly image. Like on September 16, 2021. I was mailing packages to my sister, and I noticed my sales clerk had butterfly tattoos on her right arm. So when I see them, I believe Katie is saying hello, which always brings me joy.

One particular morning back in 2016, if I remember correctly, I think this is the year. I was waking up; you know how you are sort of asleep; it's like that limbo state just before you wake up. I had this image of colored butterflies covering my face; they were all colors, even with very specific white lace and polka-dots butterflies. It was wonderful!

That morning this lovely woman from our Chicks Connect group stopped to pick me up for a day trip in Floyd Park, Las Vegas. I immediately told her what I saw. I did not know this woman, and yes, it did occur to me that she might think I had lost my mind, but I told her anyway.

When we arrived at Horses for Heroes, the management gave us a tour of an old building housed as temporary offices. It apparently was a motel from the '30s through the '60s where women could live for six weeks and get a divorce. Funny, right? Anyway, my friend followed everyone to the bathroom; it was part of the tour. My new friend came running out and said Footie, you better get in here. So, I walked in, and the shower curtain in this old bathroom was what I saw that morning in my mind. I took a photo. The pink shower curtain was filled with colorful butterflies, and yes, there were laced and polka-dotted butterflies. My only regret was I never asked to have the shower curtain. I would have paid for it or replaced it.

Now, I want to be right up front about my Kate. LOL! She was a handful! I don't want anyone to think that I am painting "my" Kate as a saint. In high school, I took a broom to her. Literally, I was screaming like a crazed woman running after her with a broom. My neighbors saw me do this, and yes, they thought I had lost my mind. They didn't know the back story. Did it make me look good? Hell no! LOL! I'm sure Katie got to school the next day and told her teachers I was a crazy mean mom. Oh my sweet tea!

This girl could rattle my nerves. Katie was always in trouble, always making up stories, and continued until she decided life was too much for her to handle. She was strong-willed, very confident, and stubborn. But I can say she loved her mom very much and told me all the time. And Katie had a heart of gold. She really would do anything for anyone who needed help. Katie reminds me of my brother Mike. Two peas in a pod. Both were broken souls who would not listen to family or friends but were extremely loved by family and friends. Katie and Mike didn't see this love because their limiting beliefs were in a different realm. Oh, my goodness, the curse of the Irish drink as my grandmother Kitty used to tell me of all our Irish relatives, especially her brothers, suffered, as she called it the Irish Curse.

At all hours, and it didn't matter what time of the day or night, I would spend time talking to Katie where apparently, well, let's say, she was out of sorts. In our early calls, I remember how I would try to give her advice or just talk, and then I realized that it didn't matter what I was saying. Katie wasn't listening. Katie's agenda was the world she was living in, and this was not a good world to be in at all. I always had to be patient no matter what time it was.

These conversations are where I would get a lot of, "I'm sorry, mom, for being such a brat," or "I now understand how you felt," or "what you were going through." Always apologizing for her past wrongdoings. It didn't matter how many times I would tell Kate she was okay. I would say to her something like, "Hey, we all gave our parents a run for their money." It didn't matter.

So I would end up being a good and, many times, a tired listener. Sometimes this would be until 2 am. Now, I would give anything to receive a crazy call from my Kate. I would give anything to hear her words. "I love you, mommy!" All I have now are photos to look at and memories. I look at Katie's picture every day and thank her for the beautiful vibes she sends me. She was so proud of me in whatever I wanted to do. She would brag to all her friends in Pennsylvania. Lord, Katie would have them friend me on Facebook.

Facebook, computers, and phones! Yikes! Katie was the only one at that time who would help me with computer stuff without giving me a "Mom!" I remember one evening my PayPal was in Chinese; oh yeah, the text was in Chinese. I thought, what the heck is happening? And when I told Katie, She got on the phone with PayPal and immediately took care of it. That was a two-hour, three-way phone call. I would never have gotten this done. No way! The poor guy on the other end didn't know what to do. LOL! Katie took control and followed through until it was fixed. When it was over, we laughed so hard, and I was so grateful. She was so smart about the business problem solving, but ask her where Spain was located. Let's leave it as your head would turn. LOL!

Another funny Katie story. I was visiting her in Texas. I spent one week with Kate and the second week with my online quilting friends for the Houston International Quilt Show. I'm trying to remember the year. I think it was 2002. I had one of those Track Phones, something the kids gave me in case of an emergency. Remember those phones? I barely knew how to use it. LOL! Anyway, One late afternoon I decided to drive to this store, Hobby Lobby, I had heard about. On the way back, I got lost and couldn't find Katie's home. It now was dark, and I was lost. So I called Kate to help me with directions. She went out of her mind! Screaming in a panicked voice. "You are in a terrible neighborhood; you need to get out of there, now!" This was repeated over and over.

By this time, I started feeling anxious and was driving in circles; at least, it seemed like I was going like a hamster wheel. Then my phone was ready to shut down because I had used up my minutes. Oh, remember those days of counting minutes. Good grief! Katie called the company and explained that I was lost and in a dangerous area with no minutes on my phone. To my surprise, they put all the minutes back on my phone to continue talking to Katie and getting back to her home. What a night! Thank goodness she was so good at figuring things out. Honestly, I don't think I was in a bad neighborhood. I was only lost.

I miss those crazy chats: the bad and the good.

It's taken years for me to mention her name and talk about "Katie" stories without going into a crying fit where the other person would feel uncomfortable.

People ask me what and how I got through my ordeal, how do I manage my life - a couple of things come to mind. One, I have the best hubby! I am lucky. He managed to keep me sane back then, and if I didn't know that this man loved me before all of this stuff. I sure did know after experiencing the worst few months of my life. He was and still is an incredible cheer-leader. He is an amazing, supportive, and loving hubby and always puts me first. Having to deal with me, my daughter's death, and a fractured ankle while I was an emotional mess. I'm not sure I could have gotten through it all without this beautiful human.

Second, my friends were doing whatever they thought would help. When I say friends, I mean friends I barely knew and some I had known forever. One adorable friend, Sally, needed fabric. God Bless her; we traveled with my stupid wheelchair to a fabric store not once but twice and off to lunch with my wheelchair. It was a humbling experience for sure. We got her fabric, and she made a fabulous bed quilt for her daughter. Amazing! She had saved all her daughter's sports T-shirts over the years and wanted to surprise her with this quilt. I embarrassed myself, crying in the car about Katie. It wasn't expected, a complete surprise I wasn't ready for, and Sally was wonderful and understanding. She listened and got me through a difficult moment.

I also remember my lovely friend Mary took me to a special event dinner with a Reiki Reader. Oh dear lord above us! I was not ready for this, and I shouldn't have attended. I drank way too much (Hubby's fault, he gave us wine before we left, LOL), and holy moly, the Reader, not knowing, was channeling Katie as Catherine to most of these women in the group. Oh yes, by the time I got to her, she looked me right in the eye and pointed her finger at my nose, and said, I can't read for you because you have been drinking.

Later this woman walked over to me and said my daughter didn't like my shoes. We all had a good laugh because, yes, Katie would have disapproved. (I can't remember anymore what I wore, it may have been my lime green converse sneakers, who knows) Anyway, several women talked about who this Catherine was because the median kept mentioning Catherine's name. I finally realized that Catherine might be my Katie. Yes, Katie is Catherine! Catherine is her birth name. So I have no idea how many hours these women talked and listened to this median to find out that she was channeling my Kate the whole time. I guess my presence was made known in that building. LOL!

And thirdly, the oils! I'm not sure why I remember this date, but on March 15, 2015, my lovely friend Lisa invited me to one of her first Doterra classes. It happened to be at a friend's house whom I absolutely adore, Zoe. She was hosting the class on this frigid evening. So the reason I emphasize these two lovely people is I would have canceled because I don't particularly care for traveling in cold, windy, snowy weather. Instead, I did it because I love both ladies and it was the best decision!

My life started to shift after this class. And I have to mention that I had no intentions of purchasing anything. Essential oils were not anything I was remotely interested in using. But, oh my goodness! So, I bought a kit and used every oil for the next six months except for the oregano. LOL! I didn't use oregano only because I never got sick and needed it, and at that time, I was afraid to cook with it.

So why was this important? The bottom line is, the oils helped me! They helped with my anxiety over losing Katie. Literally, my life felt like someone pulled out my heart as if someone pulled a rug right from underneath me. I went through every sad emotion. I felt lost and broken, and honestly, I wasn't sure how I was going to get through it. So, I was willing to give this product a try. Did I tell anyone? No? All I said was that the oils helped me with my allergies, back pain, etc. I was too fragile at the time to bring up her name without falling apart. It was easier to say I used the oils for something else.

So, I had no idea that these little gems would do so much for me. I would put a drop of Frankincense under my tongue every morning. I would diffuse it in my home. I would add a drop to my tea, and I still do this. Who knew this oil would bring me peace of mind to help me relax and feel positive, especially during those sad moments that would hit me like a ton of bricks. When you experience any sudden trauma, you never know when a backlash will occur. It comes out of the blue without warning. And honestly, I've been good, except for when and I will be honest, I was in a yoga certification course during COVID, I found myself crying all the time.

Maybe it was stress, others talking about their memories, I have no idea, but I can tell you I cried every week. And it was an awful experience to go through! The bottom line is I didn't use my Frankie! I have no idea why I stopped. Laziness! Who knows! Lesson learned! I now drink it in my tea every morning. LOL! I'm so much better.

Most importantly, I meditate and focus on being positive. Most of my life was dealing with negativity, mainly after age eight. I'm sure Kate picked up on this negativity. Life stuff is trickled down through generations. Stuff we pick up on that we don't even realize is filtering in our minds. We do what our parents did; they followed their parents, and the series is ongoing. It is like we are on autopilot. We stop and say, crap, this isn't right, but then we keep going because it is easy. Autopilot, right? We all do it, and we feel bad. Don't beat yourself up. I didn't give myself a break for years. Lord have mercy, I was a mess. A real mess!

I love how Kate reminds me she is hanging around and sending me signs. I've read seeing butterflies could be from the Universe where you are on route to an exciting journey. For example, a caterpillar evolves into a beautiful butterfly and is often seen as representing change. While others say our ancestors communicate through butterflies. Either thought is something I believe in; both ideas make me feel joyful and give me a peaceful feeling. I'm convinced seeing butterflies are signs from my Kate. Maybe you see signs?

If you have gone through the traumatic loss of someone you loved, I want my story to give you peace. I hope that sharing my story resonates with you, and hopefully, you will not feel alone. We are all in this HEALING together. I will leave you with this lovely quote.

"Even though you flew away.
In my soul, You will forever stay." - Unknown

Linda Foote

THREE

THE LABYRINTH

A JOURNEY TO WHOLENESS

"Earth our monastery
Be still and still moving
Believe only what is unbelievable."
-Unknown

I was 47, seemingly in good health, and in my 27th year of happily married life with my high school sweetheart. Christmas 2005 came and went mostly without a hitch. I say mostly because the small hitch happened on Christmas Day. My husband Brian, who always made our turkey dinners (he grew up with a special dressing recipe), forgot to turn the oven on.

When my sister and husband showed up and commented on the absence of turkey smell, Brian discovered he had failed to turn the oven on. For him to forget such an important detail was highly unusual. After some initial panic and profanity, a strategy to make up for the lost time was executed. We used the time before dinner to play games. With drinks in hand and much laughter, we finally made it to a socially late dinner. The error had left my husband a bit frazzled, and he vowed to "never make that mistake again".

We had not had an opportunity to celebrate our annual Christmas get-together and gift exchange with our neighbors Kathy and Steve. We managed to tee up a get-together for the first Friday of the new year. On my 2 km walk to work that Friday morning, I formulated a dinner plan of chicken quesadillas and a garden salad. I would walk to Bearance's grocery near work on my lunch to get the food for this spontaneous celebratory supper.

At 4 p.m., I scooped up my groceries and made the 25-minute walk home in record time. I threw the chicken in to cook and prepped the rest of the supper. My husband was in charge of picking up the libation on his way home from work. Fortunately, I still had frozen squares and cookies in the freezer that would serve as dessert. Kathy and Steve were easy company, and we had loads of fun. I am typically an organized and punctual gal, so everything was ready for their 6 o'clock arrival.

They were late, but that was no surprise. I was ready, and that was what mattered. Drinks were offered and poured, and we started to get caught up on each other's Christmas news. When my husband was asked what was new with him, to my surprise, he launched into telling our guests he had been feeling lousy and hadn't had a bowel movement since Boxing Day. I'm no math whiz, but I quickly counted about 11 days. Kathy, a nurse, said she would pop home next door and bring back some licorice tea because she thought that might help get things moving.

After an hour, there had been no movement. So, my husband excused himself and went to the pharmacy and came back with Dulcolax and two fleet enemas. The pharmacist instructed him to take the Dulcolax and, if there was no movement in a couple of hours, to take the fleet enema. If the enema didn't work quickly, a trip to the emergency might be in order.

We played games and laughed until midnight. Kathy and Steve left, and I was feeling exhausted. Brian said he would start to clean up if I wanted to head to bed and what he didn't get done, we would finish up in the morning. He kissed me and said, "If you wake up in the night, I may have taken myself to the emergency."

I was asleep before my head hit the pillow. I woke up a few hours later with a raging headache. I rarely had headaches, and I was shocked at how painful this was. It escalated to the point where I thought I would be sick. I went downstairs to get some Tylenol. On the counter, I found a note from my husband. He indeed had taken himself to emergency. I checked the bathroom and found two used fleet enema containers.

I opened the Tylenol, took two, and headed back upstairs to bed. I managed to get a few minutes of relief from the headache when I heard Brian return. He was downstairs. The headache returned and was even more painful. I felt nauseous. I stood up, and projectile vomited all over the bedroom.

I laid back down, thinking what a horrible mess that was going to be to clean up. I could feel the second round of vomit rising in my throat and wanted to get to the washroom downstairs to avoid further mess. I was aware of having difficulty managing the stairs, banging between the walls on my way down. I got to the bathroom and heard Brian say, "What's wrong with you?" I said, "I'm going to be sick." My next memory was seeing his face in mine saying, "I have called an ambulance." I remember feeling slightly embarrassed and thinking I had just had a bit too much red wine.

We only lived about 12 blocks from the hospital, and the paramedics arrived quickly. After a series of questions that I thought silly, like "What is your name?", "What year, is it?" and "Where do you live?" I was put on a stretcher and loaded onto an ambulance in frigid January temperatures. I remember playing a game in my head of, where am I now as I tried to name the street we were on and our location en route.

At the hospital, I was whisked to radiology for a head CT scan. The headache persisted. I remember recognizing the technologist as a former high school acquaintance. I felt severe panic when I was told they needed to do an enhanced CT with dye. My sister and I had taken our mother to emergency five years prior with a severe headache. Our father gave consent for the enhanced test, which revealed five brain tumors. Our mother died three months later.

I was assuming the worst. I started imagining myself in a coffin and what my eulogy might sound like. All I could think was how the love of my life would manage without me? I was wheeled back to the emergency ward, where a physician was holding my scans and my file. A face appeared over me and said, "Mrs. Rider, you have had a stroke." A lightness came over me, and I thought, well, at least I don't have cancer.

I would soon come to realize I had no idea what having a stroke meant for me. The doctor explained to my husband and I that I had had an ischemic stroke which was a blockage, and that I met the criteria to receive TPA, a drug to break up the clot. Getting TPA early is critical in having a positive outcome.

I spent the next three weeks in the neuro intensive care unit. My acute impairments were speech and walking. The stroke had occurred on the right side of my brain, leaving my left side fully impaired. I still felt as though I could walk. However, when I would try to do so, my body didn't move the way it used to. My left upper extremity was the most severely affected. Over the next three weeks, I was assessed for a possible transfer to our rehabilitation hospital, St. Mary's of the Lake Hospital (SMOL). In the short term, my swallowing was assessed daily, and I moved from liquids to pureed and finally to solid foods again.

My occupational therapist taught me the necessary strategies for activities of daily living, like ringing out a washcloth and using only one hand to wash my face, putting on a bra, and dressing. My physiotherapist worked with me, and I managed to move from a two-person assist to walking on my own. My gait wasn't pretty, but it was functional. I finally met the criteria to move to the rehabilitation hospital (SMOL), which also happened to be my place of employment before this life-changing event. On my transfer date, friends and co-workers lined the entrance to welcome me and wish me well.

I was well-liked at SMOL, and all of my potential therapists knew me. I found out later that they were all bidding to have me on their caseload. Usually, a therapist must rely on the family to get a sense of the patients' personality and abilities. Having known many of the therapists for quite some time gave me an advantage. They knew exactly what the end goal looked like; the perky brunette who raced through the halls with nice skirts and cute shoes. So once settled into my room, my boss's wife, an occupational therapist, put a huge sign on my door to remind staff, friends, and colleagues, not to over visit as it was imperative to my recovery. Repairing the brain takes an enormous amount of rest and sleep.

No time was wasted on getting me into my daily routines of speech therapy, occupational therapy, and physiotherapy. My speech at first was quiet, and I struggled with word finding. Staying focused and engaged in the activities was challenging. Two speech therapists agreed to share my case as they both wanted to help me with my recovery. I think they anticipated my sense of humor would make their job fun. I didn't disappoint. My stroke left me with no filter, and some comments from me were humorous though inappropriate.

Occupational therapy was not exactly fun. Before I could learn strategies to be functional at home and in my kitchen, I had to go through a series of tests. They were to check my cognition and memory. It became more enjoyable when I was learning how to cook again with only one functional hand. My sister often attended these sessions and made lists of the adaptive equipment I would need to be able to pull a meal together when I would eventually return home.

Physiotherapy was by far my favorite therapy, mainly because that is where I saw the most improvement. It was more like going to gym class, which was a favorite when I was in school.

I did exercises to strengthen my back, core, and legs. My left arm and hand were slow to respond or improve, no matter what the strategy.

My rehab physician explained that my brain had to make new pathways to regain functionality. I had always had a great imagination, so I started imagining new pathways forming in my brain while trying to do simple movements.

Three weeks passed, and I had progressed to a point where I was allowed a trial weekend at home to see how we would manage with me there. I was beyond excited to go to my own home, sleep in my bed, and spend time with my family, even the dog. This I how I remember it anyway. The climb to the upstairs bedroom left me exhausted. It was wonderful to be spooned by Brian and to feel safe and loved. After a great nights' sleep, I awoke the following day to find Brian standing beside me in his well-worn house coat, looking concerned. I asked him, "What is the matter?" he opened his housecoat to reveal a grotesquely swollen left leg, he was unable to put on his jeans. After a telephone consultation with my boss, a physician, he took himself again to emergency. His second visit there since the New Year, he returned home none the wiser with a plan to be called for an ultrasound the following week.

I was delivered back to SMOL on Sunday night to continue my rehab. It was an exhausting recovery and my frustration at my inability to move my left hand in any meaningful fashion had me silently crying myself to sleep some nights.

Brian had gotten his call to have the ultrasound mid-afternoon on the following Friday that I was granted another weekend pass home. The plan was for him to collect me when he was finished. My brother John and his wife had stopped to visit with me after I had finished my therapies for the day. When Brian had still not shown up by 5 p.m., John offered to drive me home. A cousin would deliver a meal for us to have that night, so I was anxious to get home. Brian would have to meet us at the house.

I was settled into the chez lounge by the fire when he arrived home. I asked, "How did it go?" He took his boots and coat off, walked over to sit down beside me, and held my hands. He said, "you won the stroke lottery, but I just found out I won the cancer lottery." I couldn't respond or even process what he had just said to me. My cousin, who was still there delivering our dinner, said some appropriate things and let himself out. My brother John looking exasperated, went out behind him. I started to feel nauseous as tears began to stream down both of our faces as we hugged and clung to each other.

After a series of more definitive testing, Brian was diagnosed with stage four lymphoma. He had a fourteen-centimeter tumor in his abdomen that touched his spleen, stomach, intestines, and bowel. His prognosis was not good. A failed start with chemo put Brian in the hospital with a lung complication for over a month.

During this time, he was an inpatient at the general hospital while I was an inpatient at the rehab hospital. Our adult daughters who were still living at home with us were doing their best to keep it together and support us. I would take the hospital shuttle bus to be with Brian when I didn't have my own therapies. Brian recovered enough to resume his chemotherapy, and I was inching closer to a discharge date in April, near Easter. My care team was concerned about me going home to be a caregiver, I was feeling good, and I knew that I had an amazing support system of family and friends. I was feeling confident about going home. Getting into a routine at home was more complicated than I thought it would be. Preparing meals with adaptive equipment was challenging. My sister dropped in almost every day to access our needs.

Another setback came for Brian, treatment was halted, and he had yet another hospital admission. I had lost my license due to my stroke, and I walked daily to and from the hospital to spend time with him. It was an emotional rollercoaster. We felt hopeful being told his tumor had shrunk, and then the consistent worsening pain revealed that cancer had spread to his spine. Chemotherapy was no longer an option, and radiation was the next thing offered, but only for pain control. That was our summer, and we seamlessly progressed into fall. Brian was able to return home; however, he was weak and thin. He was on heavy doses of morphine for pain control. We had our bed moved to the main floor bedroom as neither of us could manage just a couple of stairs, let alone a full flight without assistance. As things continued to decline, my sister came every morning to lend her support. Soon she was bringing one of her daughters.

When Brian became bowel incontinent in the nights. She and my niece would clean him and change our bedding. My non-functioning hand and arm prevented me from helping my husband. Brian had made it clear that he wanted to die at home, and I was in favor of this. I did my best at caregiving within my abilities. I wanted to appear strong and capable. I covered well the emotional toll this was taking on me. It's hard having conversations with your life partner about their impending death. Brian articulated precisely what he would be cremated in, NO SUIT. He would wear a beige pair of dockers, a maroon short-sleeved shirt with his grey cardigan. He was very specific about wearing the boxer shorts with the red hearts on them that I had given him for Valentine's Day.

Brian continued to deteriorate rapidly. In front of Brian, our palliative care physician suggested that going into the hospital palliative care would free me to be a wife and not a caregiver. Brian was in agreement with this. Brian moved into palliative care, and a cot was moved in beside him, and our daughters and I took turns staying overnight with him. Brian died within five days in my presence, our daughters, and a couple of close friends.

As far as funerals go, it was beautiful. Childhood friends of our daughter sang In Your Life by the Beatles and Hallelujah by Leonard Cohen. Our lifelong friends, Sue and Jim, did a heart-warming eulogy. As it was a December death, the congregation crossed arms, held hands, swayed to and sang Auld Lang Syne at the end of the service.

I was still healing a brain, and the first few weeks, I felt confused and could hardly make sense of the previous ten months. My eldest daughter packed up her dad's clothing and donated it to a nearby shelter. She left Brian's housecoat hanging behind the bedroom door, and I often buried my head in it to take in the last lingering scent of a life gone too soon.

Brian and I had shared a great marriage, friendship and were great lovers. I still can't explain why I started to panic about not having a life partner to grow older with. My foot still dragged, and my left arm and hand still clung to my chest, leaving me with a feeble image of myself and a sense of hope-lessness.

I kicked myself into high gear and was determined to make myself more marketable; I wanted to attract a new life partner. I know now that I moved too fast, but at the time, it felt like Brian had been gone much longer. We had been surviving and had not been a real couple in almost a year.

I got hooked up with a neuro physiotherapist who got me on a path to walking better and making my arm and hand more functional. The treatments were painful, but I was determined to be an overachiever with the exercises. It was paying off. I was beginning to gain confidence in my appearance.

Brian and I had met in high school. I was no longer going anywhere to meet anyone, so I made a profile on a dating site. I put up a current photo, but it did not show my impairments. My profile said nothing about my stroke. The first few hits were a bust. In correspondence, prospects became silent once I revealed I had had a stroke, a term now referred to as ghosting. One gentleman said I seemed like a nice woman, but he only wanted to date local women; despite his profile indicating a willingness to travel within a 400 km radius, this was a blow to my self-confidence.

I didn't open my computer for several days. When I did, there was a message in my inbox on the dating site. The photo showed a pleasant enough-looking gentleman, a Canadian, living on his boat in Trinidad. I was curious and responded. We did the preliminary getting to know each other, emails, and then I sent the email revealing my stroke. To which he replied, "and what would be the problem with that?" Feeling hopeful, I thought, maybe here's someone willing to give me a chance.

Alistair and I often talked on the phone, and I may have been slightly charmed by his British accent. He had daughters in Montreal, and he decided to put his boat up and come back to Canada to meet me. We started a romance, and he took an apartment in Kingston so he could be closer. After a short time, he moved into my home with me. He had been a sailor, and he asked how I felt about getting a boat and traveling south. After the year I'd had, I decided that a change and adventure was in order.

He sold his 45' boat in Trinidad, and I contributed to the 29' boat we bought together. We spent several months converting it to a cruising boat. It sounds luxurious, but really it was just camping on the water. It was comfortable but not glamorous.

We spent the better part of the next three years cruising the eastern seaboard and settled for several months in the Florida Keys. During this time, I made many new friends and enjoyed seeing dolphins breaching in our wake. Allister was an easy man to live with within a small space, and he took care of things that were still difficult for me. He was kind, and we were good companions. I did not love him like I did Brian. I'm not sure you ever love the same way you love your first true love.

Alistair held American, Canadian, and British citizenships. During this time, I made trips home to Canada to visit family and keep my healthcare current. Upon returning from my last visit home, U.S. customs flagged me and took me to a room. They determined I had been in the U.S.A. too long, and they would grant me a return to the boat and Allister, but only with a return date to Canada within twenty days. In Florida, Allister and I found a marina to leave the boat in while we returned to Canada, not knowing when I would be allowed to return to the U.S.A. Homeland Security could not give me an answer. I decided I would not return for at least a year.

We drove home in a rental, packed to bursting. We arrived in Kingston to live in my house. My eldest daughter, her partner, and seven pets were living in it. After a couple of days of chaos, I secured Alistair and myself an apartment, feeling it was easier for us to relocate than displacing my daughter and the menagerie.

Once we were settled in our apartment, I made an appointment for Alistair to see our family doctor for an eye problem he had developed, a shoulder problem, and urinary issues. He was seven years older than I, and I knew that prostate issues often occurred at this age. I was prepared for news regarding this.

At the doctor's appointment, the interest lay in his eye problem and an urgent appointment that day at the eye clinic. After four hours of seeing specialists and investigations, including a CT scan, we were told that Allister had a golf ball sized brain tumor. This was what had been affecting his vision. I had a sinking feeling of déjà vu. After consulting with a neurosurgeon, a surgery date was scheduled. We were cautioned of all the possible complications, but the benign, slowly growing tumor needed to be removed.

The day of surgery saw my sister steadfastly beside me. Despite ten years between us, we are very close. After what seemed an eternity, the surgeon appeared. He felt the surgery had gone well and said the tumor came out quickly despite its grizzly texture. I was able to take a peek at Al, who was still under anesthetic. The recovery nurse said it would be a while if I wanted to go home to get a bite to eat.

My sister and I returned two hours later to find that Al had been taken to radiology. He returned with the neurosurgeon, and I could tell immediately that there was a problem. Al had suffered a stroke during surgery. Because of my own experience, I didn't go into panic mode. I knew exactly what needed to be done so that he could experience that same recovery like me. I had not considered the vast differences in strokes nor their different outcomes.

This started my six years of being a caregiver. For unknown reasons, Al lacked the same desire I had to get better and continue to improve. It just wasn't in him.

At the five-year mark, I started to feel resentment. This worsened after I set up therapies to help him improve and he said, "I can't be bothered." I felt like I couldn't be bothered anymore either. My daughters were growing impatient with me, saying things like, "you need to offload him. You are way too fun to be stuck with this." While I understood their concern, I wondered if I hadn't taught them empathy and that you just don't offload someone because they were no longer fun. During my caregiver years, I started to knit again with three lovely ladies once a month, taking turns hosting.

One friend, Christine, introduced us to the labyrinth. She found it meditative and a good tool in times of uncertainty and indecision. Walking the labyrinth just made her feel better. I knew little about a labyrinth. My first walk found it a flat, circular path with many twists and turns where you finally found yourself in the center. There, one might stand in reflection or meditation. Unlike a maze, you can never get lost. As I walked it with my knitter friends, I realized it mirrored my life of twists and turns. At the center, I took a few moments to reflect. Walking back out, I could feel a sense of heaviness being lifted.

I had gotten Al to a point where he could be left alone for several hours and then to overnight alone. He could warm himself a simple meal I had prepared and left for him, but he expected me to take care of him the moment I returned. I was starting to think about what an exit strategy might look like. I found it challenging and cruel to think about, and I knew having that conversation with Al would be difficult.

Christine invited me to take a workshop with her on how to build a labyrinth. I would never build one, but she wanted to and wanted my help. I paid 95 dollars to sign up for the workshop that was to be held at cool off-grid facility called Wintergreen. A week before the workshop, Christine was hospitalized and would not be able to attend. I was uncertain about attending a workshop that I knew little about alone. It was too late to get my money refunded, and I knew the facility boasted good food.

I took the 50-minute drive that Saturday not knowing a soul. We were a small group of 10 women participants, including the attractive male facilitator. The morning started with coffee and muffins around a large round table. The facilitator, Drew, took a seat to my right. He proceeded to introduce himself as a retired minister who had built several labyrinths across Canada.

Labyrinths can be seen as religious or spiritual but are not necessarily so. After his introduction, he invited us to introduce ourselves and why we had an interest in the workshop. He started with the person to his right, making me the last person for an introduction. I listened intently to each person's introduction. Some were there for spiritual and religious reasons. A landscaper was there to expand her portfolio. Some were there out of curiosity.

My stroke had left me unfiltered at times and, for reasons I don't know, when it was my turn I started out saying, "I don't believe in God." After an awkward silence, I explained that I did think there was something bigger than us, just not as described as an older man with a beard wearing a miter and holding a staff described as God in my Sunday school class. Drew touched my arm and offered," You have grown past that image." I continued my introduction of being invited to come with a friend who couldn't make it with me.

The day was full with marking out the labyrinth and moving rocks to form the outline. Throughout the day, there was diverse chatter amongst the participants. When something was brought up about religion, I often bristled and chirped in, mostly inappropriately. Wintergreen provided a lovely lunch, and I mingled effortlessly conversing with many.

Drew approached me and suggested a coffee date to explore my chirpiness around religion at the end of the day. I said yes, thinking this could be my opportunity for an in-person "Religion for Dummies," and I could have lifelong questions about God answered.

Several weeks passed, and I was the first to reach out for this coffee date. It was fall, and I wore an orange knee-length dress and cute shoes. Drew arrived late, stating he'd had to drop his mum off at her bible study. I think I may have bristled a bit. He took my coffee order, and we did the usual getting to know you while driving. After overhearing some of my conversations with participants at the workshop, I guess he made the assumption I was married to an unwell man. Through a strained face, I told him I was, in fact, not married but had become a default caregiver to a man I had been in a relationship with. I disclosed how I wished I could find a gentle way to move Alistair out of my life and responsibility. I started the process, but it was slow going because his daughters were not keen to pick up the responsibility.

With ease, Drew moved into a ministerial counselor role and offered suggestions of how I might set myself free. We set a date for a second coffee, and this was when he asked me on an actual date to see Graham Nash at the Grand Theatre. I couldn't invite him to my apartment for dinner for obvious reasons, but I did offer to pay for our supper out before the show.

We became close friends, and he invited me to join a group of his friends for Thanksgiving at his home, a renovated barn on five acres. The path to the entrance was grass right up to the door, where dairy cattle entered and exited decades before. Behind the door was the most magical home I had ever seen. It was eclectic and leaned toward being a man cave. He had been living alone as a divorced man for over a decade. The home lacked a woman's influence. This started our romantic relationship that included long overdue intimacy. I asked him if it would be a problem that I was not a Christian, and he replied, "no, you are spiritual and have a good sense of justice."

I harbored guilt about cheating on Al even though we were long past being a viable couple. I continued with plans to move Al to Montreal to be cared for by his daughters. A series of events happened that saw Al settled in an assisted living apartment that included three meals a day. He could now sit in his recliner and watch the endless television he had become accustomed to.

Drew and I dated more freely, splitting our time between my apartment and the barn, which I lovingly referred to as the barn-dominium. I had always been a passionate gardener, and with Drew's blessing I made plans to develop a flower and vegetable garden.

Our first year saw many transformations at the barn-dominium, both inside and out. The inside started to take on a more feminine flavor, and the outside became alive with color from a flourishing garden. We continued to live separately, and I foraged ahead to expanding gardens, and we spent more time at the barn than at my apartment. March 2020, year three into our relationship COVID hit. Drew invited me to isolate myself with him to wait it out. I was happy to be in the country and not in my city apartment. As spring approached, I made more plans to expand gardens again. More soil was purchased, and many plants, seeds, and garden whimsy were collected.

I cooked great fare and set up a small bistro table near the fireplace and window. Each supper felt like we were eating at a cute restaurant. When nicer weather set in, I moved another small table with two chairs to the rock patio at the edge of the garden. Most meals were eaten there, outside, making it feel more like a vacation destination. Our meals were prefaced with gratitude. I was comfortable with this as long as it leaned towards gratefulness rather than religion. Weeks turned into months, and COVID showed no signs of receding any time soon. During an August supper where the meal had more of a Tuscany flare, Drew asked me, "would you like to live here permanently?" I knew I did, but I wanted to be mindful not to make previous mistakes. I replied, "You would have to tell me why you would like me here." After a pause, he gestured his hand towards the garden and said, "You make the ordinary, extraordinary, and none of this would have happened without you." I said I would love to stay and suggested that I give up my apartment the following April to be certain I wouldn't find the winter isolating. Of course, I knew I wouldn't feel isolated, and my heart felt full. I spent the winter planning the next garden expansion, and I poured over seed catalogs. I downsized my apartment possessions, and by the end of April, my address had been changed. Spring and summer of 2021 saw us in a new wave and lockdown of COVID at the barn.

I enjoy an early morning coffee at my garden café, where I reflect on the twists and turns in my life. In many ways, my life has been like a labyrinth. I have paralleled the labyrinth.

The universe has blessed me, putting me in my place. I thrive and connect with the earth as I never have before. I have never felt so steadfast in knowing what my future holds.

Jennifer Rider

FOUR

MY LIFE'S JOURNEY

RECOVERING FROM DRUG ADDICTION

"I understood myself only after I destroyed myself.
And only in the process of fixing myself, did I know who I
really was." - Author Unknown

I sat there, leaning up against the wishing well, calmly waiting for my mom to answer her phone. After a few rings, I heard my mom's voice "hello," I replied, "mom, you need to meet me at the hospital, got stabbed" I could hear the phone hit the floor.

At the age of 16, my life was nearly taken. My ex-girlfriend and I had gotten into an argument. It ended with me almost losing my life and her being on the run for a short while. It was a hard time, not just for my family and me, but for my friends as well, who were there and watched helplessly as it happened.

It was a long and painful journey of healing physically, and mentally, emotionally, and spiritually. I knew in my heart I had forgiven my girlfriend for what she had done. My family, though, was angry and hurt. I saw my dad cry for the first time in my life, and my mother was afraid to leave my side. My pops, thankfully, still made me laugh and held it together quite well for my family and me. I put on a mask and ignored that I was dying inside. The trauma I endured was horrible, but I felt like I had to be strong for my family.

I was offered counseling and other help more than once, but I kept refusing and saying that I was okay. But I truly believe the high doses of morphine I was on helped me stay as calm as I did while in the hospital.

It was after I was discharged from the hospital that I began to spin out horribly. The events from that day kept replaying in my head. I couldn't calm my thoughts no matter how hard I tried. I couldn't sleep for what felt like forever. My mind wouldn't stop or even slow down. Plus, watching how badly it affected my mother was destroying me.

A few short months after I was discharged from the hospital, I became very involved with my ex-boyfriend. When I started dating him, I had no idea that he was a heroin addict, but as he became more comfortable with me, he began using in front of me. My curiosity ended up getting the best of me. One day we were sitting on the couch together, and he was getting high, and I asked for some, so he gave me my first dragon.

Within seconds my mind had finally stopped racing. I felt so peaceful, so calm, so relaxed. It felt like my body had just been wrapped in a warm fuzzy blanket. At that moment, I honestly thought that I had found the cure to my PTSD, but before I knew it, I was hooked. I would wake up with cold sweats and chills, and my bones would ache. I felt nauseous. I was dope sick.

I pulled away from my family. I tried to hide the fact that I was getting high. I began lying to them often, and before I knew it, I was stealing from them too. I was skipping my probation appointments which soon landed me in juvenile detention. When I was released, I stayed clean for a short while, but I was back to chasing the dragon before I knew it. I didn't realize it at the time, but I was a full-blown addict; at the age of 17, I was court-ordered to a treatment program.

I really enjoyed my time there and learned a lot, but I wasn't ready to get clean. As soon as I graduated from the treatment program and went home, I was back out there, getting high. I continued to destroy myself and hurt those around me, but I just couldn't get clean.

It got so bad that my mom sent me to Prince George to live with my uncle Charles. And surprisingly, I was actually able to sober up for a little while.

Yes, I went out and drank here and there, which is actually how I met the father of my children. At the age of 19, I was blessed with a beautiful baby girl. I felt that things were taking a turn for the best in my life; my daughter became my whole world. Not too long after my baby girl was born, I got the news that I was pregnant again, my relationship was falling apart, and my codependency came out terribly.

I relapsed while I was pregnant with my son, and before I knew it I was single, and my daughter and I were living with my parents. Still, I continued to use, which led to my mother having to kick me out. I became homeless and stayed in shacks and on the streets. I felt so alone and broken. I was hurting my unborn child, and my baby girl was at home wondering where her mom was; to this day, when I think about that, my heart breaks. I never meant to cause my children any harm.

The disease of addiction is so cunning, baffling, and powerful. After I had my son, he was taken from me almost immediately, and that is when I really went off the deep end. I began selling my body to support my addiction, and I started hanging out with some very unhealthy people. I put myself in dangerous situations, not thinking about the consequences.

I dated men who treated me like garbage. They would lie to me, steal from me, cheat on me, and abuse me. There was one relationship I couldn't escape no matter how hard I tried and no matter how many times he almost killed me. He would beat me and anyone who wanted to help me or got in his way.

I truly believed I wouldn't escape that relationship alive after the night he stuck a loaded gun down my throat. I found a way to contact my mother a few days later, and I let her know that if I was found dead somewhere, he did it. I tried several times to leave him, but he would severely hurt everyone around me. He even tried running strangers off the road because he thought I was in their vehicle. Sadly, I had become so used to his beatings that it didn't even really scare me anymore. It was like I was just waiting for him to finally pull the trigger or beat me bad enough that I wouldn't pull through.

Thankfully I ended up back in jail and finally escaped from him. I remember how grateful I was at that time to be locked up. It's sad to say that I thought that man actually loved me, but I never really had the best examples of love growing up.

I grew up in a broken home with two parents who were pretty young when they had me, and honestly, they did the best with what they knew. They raised me the best they could. Alcoholism and drug addiction run on both sides of my family. To me, chaos was normal; I didn't know any better.

I never saw my dad take a drink. He got sober before I was born, but he had a lot of trauma he needed to heal from. He was a very hurt and broken man, and honestly, so was my mother. I watched my mother fall apart after she and my father split up. She relapsed, and before I knew it, she was deep in her addiction which meant I took on a lot more responsibility taking care of my younger siblings. I had to grow up way too fast, but in all honesty, I do not hate either of my parents because the bond I have with my siblings is strong, and I wouldn't change that for the world.

Growing up, I saw things I never should have seen or experienced, things no kid should ever have to go through, but everything that has happened in my life has shaped me into the woman I am today.

I believe my mom has been sober for about 11-12 years now, and she is the most amazing woman. She is a strong, loving, kind, and caring woman. She is the best mother and the best grandmother to my babies. My father, as well, has done much healing over the past few years. I can see that he has released so much pain. He is also an amazing man and grandfather, letting go of any anger he has been holding onto for all these years.

I have not yet mentioned my stepfather. He is also one of my biggest supports. He has taught me so much over the years, and just like my mom and dad, he never gave up on me.

He and my mother used to come and find me when I was in my active addiction to check up on me and remind me that they love me, and before they would leave, they would always say, "We love you, and when you are ready we will be here."

I held onto that always, and when I was finally ready, they were right there like they promised. I have three loving parents who I kept up at night worried that they would get a call that I died. I lied to them, stole from them, worried them sick, and lashed out at them. Not once did they hold those things over my head. They forgave me and loved me, and supported me through it all. I am truly grateful for being sober today because my parents can sleep at night knowing their daughter is okay.

In June 2019, I was arrested for the last time, and is when I finally decided to sober up.

I was back in jail again after promising my family and my babies that I wouldn't go back there. I made so many broken promises. The last time I was so full of shame and guilt that I knew I couldn't keep going on like that anymore. I was tired of hurting my family and myself. When I made those promises to my family, I really truly meant it. But because I wasn't dealing with the trauma that led me to use in the first place, I would always go back.

When I first got locked up, the last time, I was going through the worst withdrawals I had ever gone through. I assaulted the guards, and of course, I was thrown into segregation. After being in there for a few days, I was in horrible shape. I couldn't eat or drink anything. I was rushed to the hospital, and I ended up spending a few nights there getting fluids through an intravenous.

Once I got back to the jail and out of segregation, I started taking the steps I needed to find a recovery house or treatment center. I read up on several different ones until I found the perfect one for me. It was a year or longer, which is what I knew I needed. I filled out the paperwork, and it got sent out. After a short while, I was accepted into the program.

I would be lying if I said I wasn't nervous or scared, because I was scared shitless! I had no idea what to expect. The fear of the unknown was overwhelming. When I got picked up from the jail by some of the staff from the recovery house, I felt relieved. They were so kind and welcoming, and when I got to the house, the house manager said something to me that has stuck with me since "I will love you until you can love yourself."

My first couple of weeks at the house were extremely hard. A part of me wanted to run away and use drugs so I could be numb again. Still, there was a part of me that really wanted to stay because I was sick of slowly killing myself and destroying everyone around me. Thankfully the part of me that wanted to stay was stronger than the part of me that wanted to run.

Learning to face my problems instead of run away from them was probably one of the hardest things I learned how to do because, for years, I didn't know how to live without putting a substance into my body. With the guidance of other women and my higher power, I learned how to let my walls down. I learned how to feel again without wanting to run. I even knew how to identify what emotions I was feeling. I worked through trauma, guilt, shame, and resentments that I had been carrying with me for years.

I have forgiven those who hurt me, and most importantly, I have forgiven myself. I learned a new way of life. I grieved the girl I used to be because that girl is gone now, and I will never be her again, nor do I want to be! Every day I am learning new things about myself, and I can happily say that most days, I love myself. I still have days that my past comes up, and it can be overwhelming, but I allow myself to feel and process those things as they come up,

I have freedom today; I no longer have to run away!

I get to help other women today who are struggling and also trying to find their way. I have people who show up for me today, and I get to show up for others as well. I have a relationship with my family and my two beautiful children. I have been blessed with so many gifts on my journey, being able to visit my children and my family, my charges were dropped, and I could get and keep a job.

I was also blessed with another family, my recovery family. I get to help others, which I have always wanted to do, and I will be starting a new job that I have wanted to do for quite some time now.

I have built a strong, trusting, and loving connection with my creator (higher power) and also myself. I have learned to be loving and tolerant to even those I do necessarily like or get along with.

My life, even in recovery, has had a lot of ups and downs. I would be lying if I said things were amazing all the time, but today I am genuinely grateful for the struggles I go through. I learn from them, and they help me appreciate the good moments in my life so much more.

I do not regret anything I have gone through in my life because I am the woman I am today because of those experiences, and I get to share my experience with others today and help them. I am not a victim of the abuse I went through; I am a survivor, and I am also a survivor of my addiction.

I overdosed so many times, but thankfully my creator had another plan for me. Today, I am not afraid to ask for help and offer a helping hand to those struggling.

I just need to say I am grateful to my family for never giving up on me, for the women who loved me before I could love myself and for those who have walked this path of recovery before me, and to my boyfriend, who gave me a nudge to write and share my story.

If you are struggling in the ways I was, please know you are not alone. There is help for you, but you must reach out to ask for it. No one can do it for you. That was a big lesson I had to learn, that I was responsible for my addiction and that I was responsible for my recovery.

There is an amazing life waiting for you.

Kari Baxter

FIVE

UNCONDITIONAL LOVE AND HOW I FOUND IT

HOW I BUILT MY FAMILY

"I carry your heart. I carry it in my heart"
E.E. Cummings

On a warm August day in 2003, at the age of 42, I was going over my finances and decided to make a change to my phone bill. Why was I paying an extra $4.00 each month to have my number unlisted? It made no sense at all. I made the call to the phone company to take me off the unlisted numbers and have it listed the next day. One day after work, I arrived home to find a message left for me. I did not recognize the Alberta number as I pressed play on my answering machine. Little did I know then, but that message would change my life.

As a single mom to three daughters, I had always worked full time. It was summer break and the night I played the message,

I had my youngest daughter by my side. I listened and then called the number that was left. A woman answered, told me her name and where she was calling from. She then asked me a few things about myself; where was I born and what year? Then she paused, a long pause, before she said, "Oh my God! I found you!" I asked, "Who's looking for me?" She said, "Your birth father!" I was stunned!

Before I continue, I'd like to tell you that I was placed into the Alberta foster care system at birth. I had been surrendered at a hospital in Edmonton and shortly after, I was placed into a loving Catholic home. My foster parents are white, I am Chipewyan Cree. Growing up though, I'd tell people that I was Metis as I honestly did not know of my origin back then. I later discovered that it was my birth mother's wish to have me placed into a Catholic home. I had read a social worker's report from back then and it also stated that my birth father knew of my mother's condition and he wanted nothing to do with me. And I believed those words up until that fateful day. The papers had also spelled his last name incorrectly.

It turned out that the person who had called me, was in fact my cousin! She said that my father had enlisted her to help him find me. He knew where and when I was born but that was the only information that he had. At the age of about one, my foster parents had moved us to B.C.

I later discovered that both of my birth parents came from the same small remote northern community in Alberta. My cousin went on to say that they'd heard through the grapevine that I could possibly be in the Prince George area. This was true of course, but because I had an unlisted number, her search came to a halt. And then I had it listed. Two days, it was two days after I had it re-listed, that she found my number. But my father, Charlie Voyageur, had been searching for me my whole life!

After the shock of hearing of his search, I was completely overwhelmed. I did not know what to do next. During my conversation with my cousin, she said she had to make some calls and that she would call me back in 15 minutes. Forty-five minutes later and I was a mess, sitting and waiting for the call. So, I did what I always do when I am feeling lost; I called my Mom.

Having been raised by my foster mother my entire life, she is simply, Mom to me. I called her and told her what had happened. She was just as flabbergasted as me. I was freaking out and my daughter was trying to figure out what was going on with me. Poor little thing. She and her sisters had never seen me cry before and that was my choice. As a single mom, I wanted too always be strong for them.

I jumped out of my skin when the phone rang. It was my cousin, and she was telling me that she had sent her daughter over to pick up my father so he could talk with me. I said, "Now?!?" I was panic stricken. And then he spoke. "I've been looking for you for a long time" he said. And then I lost my shit. I felt like I was on an episode of Oprah, you know, the ones where families are reunited. I couldn't stop crying. And then I looked over at my daughter. She had the strangest look on her face, as if to say. "What's wrong with my mom and why are her eyes watering?" After finally composing myself, we were able to have a conversation. He told me how he searched for me every time he was in Edmonton.

My father had been a diamond driller and had travelled the world for his work; from Africa to Australia, all over the States and in Canada. Each time he was able to, he'd go to Edmonton as that was the last place where he knew I had been. I later found out that on one trip there, he ran into my birth mother. He said he was so excited to see her and asked her if she knew where I was. Unfortunately, she was no help at all. She was so drunk that he could not understand anything that she was saying. He kept asking about the baby, the baby, but nothing came of it. Again, he was at a loss.

Our conversation continued with many questions. I discovered that I was his only child. In response to that, I was only too happy to tell him that he had three granddaughters! I swear, I could almost hear his smile. Granddaughters! And not just one but three! By the end of that first conversation, arrangements were being made for all of us to be flown there for Christmas that year and it would be paid by the Band, to which I now belong. We'd get to meet our family and our community and see where my parents were from. As both of my parents were from the same place, I also managed to meet relatives from my birth mother's side of the family.

Getting to meet my dad and hugging him, there was no greater feeling of love, security and belonging. I felt like I belonged. I attended Midnight Mass with him and during the service, we had to hold hands. I instantly felt like his little girl, holding his hand, and feeling so safe.

We had several visits through the years; sometimes in Edmonton, once in Fort St. John and once when he came to see me and my family here in Prince George! By that time, there was a great grandson for him to meet, who had been given my dad's name as his middle name. When my second grandchild was born, I took both her and my daughter to visit my dad at his home. This time, they held a gathering at my father's home where the community had pulled together and gifted my daughter with a very large sum of money to help with her new baby girl. They were all so happy for my dad. They wanted to celebrate his having a child, grandchildren and great grandchildren.

While on our first visit in 2003, my Voyageur cousins asked me if I wanted to meet my birth mother's mother. What??? Yes please! So off we went, driving over the winter road up to Fort Smith. I knew of my grandmother, but I didn't know that my mother was her favourite and when she saw me, her eyes lit up.

By then, grandma had trouble communicating and didn't speak much. She just kept looking at me. It was a brief visit and as I left to follow my cousins out to the parking lot, I stopped and turned around. I realized that I probably would never see my grandmother again, so I went back into her room. She looked so sad, sitting in her bed. I went to her, hugged her, and told her I loved her. She hugged me so hard and said she loved me too. My heart felt light, and I knew I had made the right choice to go back to see her. She died the next spring.

By about 2006, I began the process of legally changing my last name to my father's which of course, is Voyageur. I had had my birth mother's last name, then my husband's and finally, the one I should have had my whole life. Shortly after that, I obtained my Status and am now proudly a member of the

Athabasca Chipewyan First Nation from Fort Chipewyan, Alberta.

By October of 2017, my father was dying. I was flown to Edmonton to be with him. He was in a coma by then and my family said he was waiting for me. As I held his hand, I leaned close to him to say, "Dad, I'm here. Can you feel my hand? I love you Dad." By then, I was crying uncontrollably. My family took me back to the hotel and I tried to sleep. Within a couple of hours, the call came for us to hurry back to the hospital.

We got to say our final goodbyes, and then he was gone. We had 14 years of phone calls, visits, and letters. I don't know if he ever really knew how much he changed my life. I still look for him in pictures that are posted from our community there. Funny thing is, I know I always will.

In his memory, I now have three tattoos. One shows the words, Charlie's Girl along with the year he was born and the year he died, the second is of the emblem from my Band and the third is of a feather that encompasses one side of the first two. I want people to ask about them so that I can tell them about my great father.

In November of 2017, a change was made in Fort Chipewyan and the Charles Voyageur Conference Centre was unveiled. My father had lived in his community for most of his life. As an Elder, he created and built a Youth Camp for the young people in Fort Chipewyan to learn outdoor survival skills, hunting, fishing, and how to do trapping. My dad had a trap line set out over many miles and, back in the day, would take his dog sled out to check the trap line for any animals he may have caught. This process would take weeks at a time, all done during the winter. The skills he acquired through the years were passed onto the youth. He'd lived off the land, hunting, fishing, and foraging. People in Fort Chipewyan all knew who Charlie was. His vast knowledge of the land and of his people made him a very wise, well known and well respected Elder.

The day after my father died, arrangements were made for his funeral, for my flight to Fort MacMurray, and, for my daughters to join me there. I felt complete having them by my side. We were briefed on what we could expect over the next few days. There was the viewing in Fort MacMurray, then the flight to Fort Chipewyan where the whole community was waiting. They loaded my father's coffin into our small plane, and we set off.

We flew over the place that he grew up in called Jackfish and then we circled Fort Chipewyan twice so the people waiting could see we were bringing him home. I said to my daughters, "If you ever wanted to know what it feels like to be a celebrity, this is it." Our plane was met by dozens of people who embraced us. The procession into town was endless. Someone whispered to me, "Turn around." All I could see were car lights behind us, as far as the eye could see. A three-day wake ensued, complete with so much food and also entertainment performed by relatives and guests. There was always someone with my dad, day, and night. In all my life, I had never experienced that type of a funeral. It was amazing, wonderful, sad and happy too. Seeing so many people who loved and respected my dad was a comfort to me.

Through the years, I usually spent Christmases with my mom and stepdad. On one of those visits, the phone rang and it was my dad. Mom answered the call and I remember her saying, "I bet you want to talk with our daughter, Charlie." I never thought of it that way, but it was true. I was their daughter.

My mom, she is the shit! Five foot nothing, 110 pounds soaking wet and full of piss and vinegar. She raised not only me, but also my older half brother and two other boys. We have all remained with her our whole lives. All of us are part Aboriginal. Mom had experienced fertility issues for several years and just wanted to be a mother.

She eventually did have two children of her own, but well after we had all arrived into her life. My foster father had mental health issues that went undiagnosed for many years. Mom couldn't take it anymore, so for her safety, as well as ours, we left our father. I was 16, going on 20. To say I was a handful would be an understatement. I used to say to myself, if I ever have a daughter, I hope she is nothing like me as a teenager. Boy, was I lucky in that respect.

After failing grade 10, I repeated that grade and went on to graduate. I couldn't have done it without my mom's unending support and love. I also made many bad choices along the way. I got pregnant not once but twice and all by the time I was 20. The first time I got pregnant, I was 17 and in grade 11. I had a therapeutic abortion. The second time, I had just turned 20 and had planned to have the baby. This was not to be. My mom convinced me to seek another abortion as there was no father involved and I was still living at home. I had no job and no means to care for a child. She knew I had seen and done things no teenager should ever have to go through.

On July 3rd, 1976, I was a witness to a fatal car accident, been gang raped that same day, went through an inquest that September because of that accident and came through the other side with my mom right next to me. (The story of this accident made national news and would later be made into a book by Bridget Moran, titled, Judgment at Stoney Creek).

The accident happened after a street dance in Vanderhoof. I was with a group of people and we were just walking up a street from downtown. By the time we were headed up the hill out of town towards a Reserve, another group of people were nearby. That group of Aboriginal girls were walking home and for whatever reason, the group I was with began name calling and shouting insults. Then, somehow it was decided that each group would play 'chicken' with the cars as they drove by. Why? I never knew why. As a car drove past my group, they were passing the other group and from where I stood, I saw one of the girls take a big step forward. The car never had a chance to slow down. It struck her instantly, leaving her lying on the pavement, one sandal thrown several feet away in the road. A nearby neighbour heard the commotion and came to help. He brought out a blanket to cover the girl and it was then that I saw her pregnant belly. Oh no, I thought. This can't be happening! She died in front of me. When the police finally showed up, we all had to give our names as witnesses and would later go to the police station to give our statements.

After the accident, I continued walking with a group of boys, one of whom was my boyfriend at the time. By now it was about 6:00 or 7:00 in the morning. At one point, my older brother and his friend appeared. Someone showed up in a car and we all hopped in, or so I thought. As we drove away, I looked back for my brother and he was still on the street walking. But I felt safe knowing my boyfriend was with me. After driving to a remote spot on the outskirts of town, we pulled into a field. I still felt safe, but maybe then, not so much as earlier. Before I knew it, I was being held down, my clothes were taken off and the gang rape began. There were six of them, all taking turns. I tried fighting back, screaming and kicking but to no avail. There were too many of them. I even pretended to faint but it didn't matter by that point. After what seemed like hours, they let me get dressed, brought me back into town and let me go home. As if my life hadn't gone for shit by witnessing someone die, I now had to deal with my gang rape.

When I told my parents, they were in shock. I was only 14 at the time. The police were called and I attempted to make yet another statement. When they found out one of the boys was a boyfriend and I had willingly gotten in the car and, what I believe, saw I was native, they told my parents not to bother with charges. They said my name would be 'dragged through the mud' and nothing would come of it. Nothing! And so, nothing was ever done. There was so much racism in that town, it was terrible.

Now, 45 years later, that horrible day can still make me sad, frightened and feeling hopeless. It could have easily taken over my life, but I chose to continue moving forward, making plans with my family and enjoying this life I have built.

The inquest followed in September of that same year. It was held at my high school in the small gymnasium. The 'witness room' was just a classroom. No family was allowed, so it was just me. Oh! And of course, my rapists as they were witnesses. I sat alone, frightened to death and I had to listen to them talking about their great night with me along with sneering and laughing. I was so scared; I actually broke out in hives!

The inquest itself was to determine if the accident was just that, an accident.

Two years prior to this, someone else had also died on that same stretch of road, hit and killed by the brother of the accused driver. The other victim was related to the victim that I saw die. It was such a mess. There were so many lawyers, people from the press, cameras and of course, curious onlookers seated in the gym that day. When my turn came to sit at the witness stand, I was made to feel small and weak. I wanted to run out of the gym. In the book, Judgment at Stoney Creek, I was described as the native girl who was with the white guys. I decided if I could get through the rest of high school, start fresh somewhere else after graduation, do my best to move on with my life, then that was what I would do and I did! With determination and a good support system, anything is possible.

Without my mom's love and support, I wouldn't have gone on to attend college, find a job and a place to live in Prince George. But then, I became pregnant again. This time was different. There was no way I would ever have another abortion. I knew I wanted to be a mother. Having my daughter at the age of 23 on my own, saved my life. Having her made me look at my life and see what I needed to change to make a good life for her and be a good provider. I tell my 36-year-old daughter, Rayelle, that she is my hero for saving me from a life headed down the wrong path. If I hadn't had her, would my life have taken a wrong turn? Would I have become an alcoholic or addicted to drugs? Knowing that this little person was wholly dependent on me, gave me a reason to be a better person and a loving mother, just like my mom.

Around 1987, a new program was being launched for single mothers through Social Services and I was asked to join it. From there I began my career, working for lawyers. I was able to provide for my child and myself. What a great feeling! I then met my husband, had another daughter, Sara who is 31 and thought life couldn't be better. But life had a different plan for us. I left my husband, started a divorce and then discovered I was pregnant. I knew I would have my third child, a daughter I named Claire, who is now 28. It was the best decision of my life. My little family was complete.

In 1992, about the time of my divorce, it was revealed that my birth mother had had other children after she had had my older brother and me. Seven more to be precise. In March of 1992, my brother and I flew to Edmonton to meet three of them. The similarities were endless. Since then, I've met all but one of my newfound siblings. As our mother had more children, she also drank during those pregnancies. I was so saddened to learn that some of my siblings suffer from fetal alcohol effects and syndrome. Of the nine of us, I am the only one to have finished high school and also to have some post secondary education.

In 1996, I met my soulmate. Kelly was my world. He loved my children like his own. Having him in our lives enriched it in many ways. I had become a member of his wonderful and amazing family and he was a welcomed member to mine. When we became grandparents, he was in his element. I loved watching him with our grandson. He'd take him everywhere for their adventures.

When our granddaughter was born, he was so happy, he wept. He was their papa and they were his grandchildren. It didn't matter that they were not blood. In 2014 though, he and I decided to go our separate ways but we both knew we would always be best friends. We shared in the love of our daughters and grandchildren.

In 2018, our world came crashing down. Kelly was diagnosed with terminal cancer and given 18 months. September 22nd, 2021 marks one year since we lost our dear Kelly. Besides my own daughters, I wish to dedicate this chapter to him. He loved to hear over and over, how my dad found me and every time he did, he'd cry. He made sure that I got to Fort St. John when my dad went there for a conference. In Kelly's final months, he wanted to move back to Prince George. I managed to find him a place in my apartment building. He moved in on the 4th of July, 2020 and was gone in September, just over two months later.

On his final night with us, my daughters and I sat around him. Kelly was heavily drugged by then and had stopped talking a few days prior. My daughters and I were talking about the good old days and then one of my girls played a song on her phone and placed it close to his ear. We continued chatting away and then I saw a tear trickling down his face. I knew he felt us there and heard a favorite song playing. What a great memory for us.

Kelly's family were all there that night. It was so special for me to be a part of his loving family. They have always treated me like one of their own and I am eternally grateful for them. I sat with his sister until he took his last breath. A phrase came to me while sitting there watching Kelly. "Waiting for a death is like waiting for a birth." And then he was gone. That was when I let my tears flow. I hadn't let myself cry before then because I wanted to be strong for my girls.

When my baby brother visited Kelly just days before his passing, I made sure I was with him. He and Kelly were very close. My brother couldn't contain his sadness and wept in to my arms. I was glad that he had asked me to accompany him that day. I wanted to be there and to be strong for him. Kelly died in the same room at Hospice that his mother died in several years before. We knew he would be joining his parents and friends who had passed before him. I feel his presence all the time. I know he keeps an eye out for me. I know it when I hear a song he loved, see his favourite baseball team on the television and watch our grandchildren grow. Now we have another grandchild joining us in January. How I wish she could meet her papa Kelly. He would have loved her so much.

Through it all, it has always been my mom who kept me grounded, kept me sane, kept me safe, loved me unconditionally and never made me feel like I didn't belong. She is always the one I look to for guidance. She's my biggest cheerleader. When I think back on all that she has been through in her 83 years, I am in awe of her strength. But when Kelly died, we cried together.

Mom is one of eight children and is the oldest daughter. She married at 18 and left to start her own family. When her mother died in an accident, she went back home to help care for her younger siblings.

My mom had fertility problems and after five years of marriage, decided to put her name in to be a foster parent at the urging of her neighbor. Shortly after, I was placed in her care, quite unexpectedly. She had nothing ready for me and wasn't able to call my foster father at his job to tell him. Instead, she had placed me on their bed and when he got home from work, she sent him into their room and asked him to see what was different. He came out of the room and said, "You put a new bedspread on?" He didn't even see me! My "crib" that night, was a dresser drawer. And when I had my first daughter, I left the hospital and took her to my mom's, where she lovingly placed my baby into a dresser drawer for her first night at her grandma's home.

When I was almost 10, mom had her first biological child. I was over the moon with excitement and happiness! I prayed for a sister as I already had three brothers. When my sister was born, I was beyond happy. I was then referred to as her 'second mom'. I'd do anything to help my mom. When my youngest brother was born two years later, it was just mom and us kids. She was raising all six of us on her own and she did the best job! We never wanted for anything. I knew then that I wanted to be just like her when I grew up. Growing up in Ladner, I had my mom's siblings and their children to spend time with.

One cousin in particular became my favorite. We spent many summer days, weekends and holidays together. She became like a sister to me and I am eternally grateful to her for always being my sounding board, my mentor and my best friend. There's a saying that goes, "a cousin is like having your first best friend" and it is so true. For my 60th birthday this summer, my beautiful cousin flew me to Ladner to visit. It was like my best dream come true. I always wanted to drive around and see the places I remembered; the pool, library, my old school and the Church I had attended. Being raised Catholic, my first six years of school were at Sacred Heart. If not for my cousin, none of this would have been possible. It was wonderful to catch up and talk about our childhood. I love her so much.

In closing out my chapter, I would like to say how honored I am to have been asked to join this amazing group of women authors. In telling my story, I can show how I have grown into the woman I have wanted to be since I was a little girl. Watching and learning from my mom has given me a strong foundation. She has shown me how to love, care, be kind and generous. Also, what it takes to be a good listener, that shoulder for someone to cry on and to have empathy for those who need it, to never judge anyone and above all, to be honest. These are cherished gifts that my mother has given me. My mom is a mother to 6 children, grandmother to 18 and a great grandmother to 9, soon to be 10.

When I think back to how I have lived, both the good and the bad, I always ask myself, where would I be without my mom? Who would I have become? Would I have this life that I love, surrounded by people who love me? Thanks to my mom, I have all of these things. She used to tell me that I had not grown under her heart, but in it. And thank you to Charlie, my birth father and to my birth mother, June, without them, I wouldn't even be here! Also, thank you to my foster father, Raymond who taught me to laugh, be silly, tell old jokes and love Chinese food. He was my hero. Then there's my awesome stepdad, who married my amazing mom with her six children He's a biker with a heart of gold. He continues to keep mom on her toes and all of us kids in line. Nothing gets past him. And we love him all the more for it.

Always be grateful for family and for the love you receive from them. It's that love that keeps us moving forward and keeps our feet planted firmly on the ground. I have learned that we get in return, what we put out into the world. Take nothing for granted. It doesn't matter how you have built your family because with family, comes love. Without love, what is there?

Michelle Voyageur

SIX

ADHD & ME

DAILY STRUGGLES

"I'm different and that's ok." - Crystal Marcoux

Imagine being five years old sitting in a kindergarten class and the teacher constantly asking you to sit still, focus, and stop talking, but no matter how hard you try, your body just won't stop. It feels like there are surges of energy running through it, and your mind is thinking of 30 things all at once.

Kids are constantly making fun of you for how much you talk, and every time you try and help, it's always taken the wrong way. Your parents take you to see a specialist, and you get a diagnosis of ADHD. However, even after knowing what's wrong with yourself and taking medication and lifestyle changes your parents did for you, you still felt different from everyone else; you were alone and not understood.

Every day you would sit in class looking around at all the other kids, not understanding why everything the teacher was saying seemed to resonate with them, and you just sat there feeling lost and stupid.

Jump forward to seventeen now; after continuing to have these feelings and struggling throughout school, you come across your first colossal life lesson. You got tired of being ashamed of a diagnosis and watching those around you who are going through the same thing hold their heads down, hide who they are, afraid to ask for help. It was then that you realized that if you wanted to move forward, you needed to change yourself as only I have the power to change me," that's when the shift happened.

You finally embraced the learning style that worked for you and the way you learn, absorb, and apply what you've learned. Finally, you started asking for help and you finally changed from a D average student to an A/B average. You began to search within yourself, at what strengths you have and realize your biggest is the ability to help and understand others. With this newfound thought, you decide to continue on a post-secondary education journey.

In 2006 you graduated with distinction from the health care assistant course. While taking this course, you could've gone to the learning aid classroom and sat with teachers who help students with learning challenges. Instead, with your newfound realizations there in the back of your head yelling out, you decided to keep moving forward, constantly repeating in your head, "I only have the power to change me." In the end, after going into this course with an amazing attitude, you completely embraced what made you different and let your strengths show.

You graduated with distinctions which were only possible after accepting all of your challenges and how you learned, then taking steps to speak up and talk with all the instructors about your struggles with learning, and together they helped you succeed. This isn't saying that it wasn't hard. You had to apply yourself 100% and be in constant communication with your instructors while battling those who bullied and doubted you. Bullies who were saying, "why bother going to college? You're just going to fail." Once you receive any type of learning challenge, especially ADHD, you're instantly labeled, and people just don't understand.

On top of that, you constantly fight within yourself, doubting yourself, too scared to try and fail because you then prove everyone right. For the majority of your life, trying to change yourself into someone you weren't to make everyone around you happy. As every time you'd let the real you show, people would laugh at or make fun of you, people would stop being friends with you and constantly being told, "sorry, you're just too much for me."

You're 27 and 4 years into a new career where you feel and know the difference that you wanted to make is happening while still feeling constantly misunderstood by your peers. When you look normal on the outside because your challenges all come from within, people constantly judge and ridicule you as they just don't understand or are just ignorant.

However, you've become very comfortable explaining your challenges to those around you at this stage in life and try your best to help them understand. This being said, adults can be very cruel, and some still choose to be ignorant and continue to place roadblocks in front of you. You must accept and understand that every person's put in front of you for a purpose. You must figure out how to change our own response, reaction, or choice.

In April 2010, a new fear and challenge were placed before you, even though it'd be the only life goal you feel you haven't accomplished yet, becoming a mother. So many thoughts and emotions were going through your head around becoming a mother. Once again here comes the opinions of others questioning your capability of being a good mother with all the challenges placed before you.

Two years later, being blessed with a second son and taking the steps to remove the three of you from an unsafe situation, and now becoming a single mother of two boys who are unaware of the challenges that would be placed upon them as they get older.

When these boys were five and three years old, they were both diagnosed. The oldest has ADHD and ODD (Oppositional Defiance Disorder), and the youngest with Impulsive ADHD, ODD, Sensory Processing Disorder, Anxiety, and waiting on a Turrets and Autism assessment. Since their diagnosis, our lives consist of working full time and attending many doctor's appointments, assessments, parenting courses, counseling, and trying to make great memories with the children.

In 2018 was the welcoming of a beautiful baby girl and gaining an amazing four-year-old stepson and now having four beautiful children. You end up going through many struggles with your daughter's health to find out she has Hypotonia Syndrome and Bethlem Myopathy.

In February 2021, your stepson comes to live with the family full time, and you learn that he also has learning and behavior challenges. So now, you are faced with having your own challenges, both mentally and physically, to deal with and four beautiful children with their own challenges that need your guidance and care.

On the one hand, you understand where the boys are coming from as there are many similarities with your brain functions, but on the other hand, you struggle with being able to keep yourself composed and do right by the kids at times. Even being on medication, you still experience struggles. The biggest struggle is impulsivity which can get the best of you and reacting the wrong way at times with the children. This ends up filling you with guilt and pain, which you beat yourself up about.

Eventually, getting to the point where something has to give, or you're not going to be able to be the parent these children need. All the courses being taken have significantly helped; however, having the type of brain you do applying a lot of the skills that were being taught were more difficulty than they should be.

Again, that stigma about learning challenges and all those people who doubted your parenting ability were right there inside your head, and you ended up freezing and couldn't reach out and ask for help. Resulting in you becoming very short with the children and being that parent who yells not talk it out to their kids. Things that weren't a big deal started becoming a big deal, and you could see your kids didn't enjoy your company or want to do things with you.

One day finally, you woke up and took a good look at what you were becoming and remembered what helped you make that big life switch years ago. "I only have the power to change me". You then decided to go back on medication and start talking to someone about your struggles as a person and parent. Then you started focusing on yourself and not everyone else.

Everything slowly shifted in every way, and life slowly started falling into place. Once you accepted that "I'm different and that's ok" and embraced who you are as a positive, not a negative, your strengths outweighed your weaknesses, and you started making even more of a difference.

You then started to teach the children that everyone makes mistakes, even parents. It's how you respond to the mistake that makes the difference.

In our house, the words normal and perfect aren't allowed. These are worse than using a swear word, as nothing is ever perfect. You can also show improvement, and no one is normal. We are all unique in our own way. I believe when people use these two words, you will always set your children up to fail because these are unrealistic. Every day people will be placed in front of you to challenge you, and ignorance will always be around.

Unfortunately, there will always be stigmas around any disability, but I believe the more we speak up and ask for help, the more this will change for the better. Your hesitation was there because of how people look at you. Once you get labeled, and every time you stayed quiet, there were negative outcomes. Once you had the courage to speak up and ask for help, things changed for the better.

This being said, you continue to work hard every single day to achieve the daily goals set for yourself and to be the parent your children need and want, but you love yourself wholly now. "It's ok to be me. If I love me, then I accept me for me. I only have the power to change me".

I'm now 38 years old, and I love and accept myself completely. I'm able to accept all other individuals I come across in my life and how they're going to see or deal with myself and my children and not take it to heart or personally, and it's ok for them to be that way.

Not everyone is meant to understand us. I've got a loving man who's been with me for almost five years, and between the two of us, we've got four beautiful children who are so unique. Each brings a different spark to my life, and all of them give me the strength to keep moving forward as I watch them persevere through their daily struggles their challenges bring them.

I've had the same health care job for 15 years now and love going to work and bringing my unique heart and compassion to touch so many people at my place of work on a daily basis. I truly believe that if I wasn't blessed with having impulsive ADHD, I wouldn't be able to be who I am and do what I not only do at work with those around me but also the mother and partner I am. "I am me because of the great gifts I was blessed with that makes me unique and one of a kind."

My message for you reading my story is this, "None of us are the same, we are all different, and that's the way it should be. Imagine how boring our world would be if we were all the same. Love yourself for your uniqueness and love yourself for being you. Because you are amazing just the way you are."

Crystal Marcoux

SEVEN

SHATTERED

HOME OF THE UNWED

"She dipped her wings in ink to cover up her scars & wrote her story in the sky. Her words lit up like stars. ~ Christy Ann Martine

This story of my journey has been hidden for a very long time. It was a chapter in my book of life that had been torn out, then buried & hidden ~ but never lost. As hard as I wanted to lose this story, it followed me like a shadow. Adding a deep, tainted despondency to everything I touched. As much as I wanted it to be gone- it was here.

So I made a bargain ~ I, with genuine fortitude, banished this story to only the darkest parts of me. I wrapped chains around it, was disgusted by it, ashamed of it, and firmly expressed that whatever punishment it got was well deserved. It was NEVER to see the light of day!

Little did I realize that whatever damnation I placed upon it, I was placing on me.

One of the first places I shared this story was on a retreat during my last weekend of training before being initiated as a high priestess. We did what is called Circle many times during this weekend. The circle is a very healing place – it was a very special but extremely soul-wrenching weekend, where we went deep into the depths of our personal shadows.

This story emerged with an urgency to come out. It was something I had purposely kept in the darkest corners of my mind, soul, and being, and there was still much shame around this part of me. I had been avoiding looking at it, but there was a soul, a fellow sister, in this particular weekend circle that needed to hear it. She needed to find healing in it, and I remember as I told it, we locked tearful eyes and swirled together in our mutual pain.

I felt the fires of Kali, the goddess rising as she stripped me of this agony and stomped on the pain and stopped both of us in our tracks of any further self-loathing and the need to rehash, relive and repeat our hurt and pain in the most destructive ways. Until that moment, I realized I had not been healing but allowing myself to be a victim over and over again.

Kali gave me the strength and courage to share my story - to bring it to the light of her fires so it may be used to provide light, safety, and healing for others. I had held onto it long enough. It is not in my sacred contract to keep it to myself - It was given to me to share and help others heal ~ not to keep it for my own, as I had been. My pain would help others know they are not alone in their darkness. My pain was a gift that allowed me to speak the very special language of those who are suffering a special kind of pain and – as someone who understood how to not only survive but heal and grow and walk proudly again, after a... Rape.

I have this knowledge because at the age of 16, walking home one night from a party, I was raped. I'm going to use this word because "sexually assaulted" isn't a strong enough word. I was attacked, beaten up, knocked unconscious, and raped. When I came to, I was on the ground. I could feel the rock that had knocked me out digging into my head, pressing on the soft, bruised spot it had created. My pants and underwear had been pulled down around my ankles.

As I was slowly gaining my vision back, I realized that my rapist was "finishing up". I had so much pain coming at me from so many places, on and in my body, but my brain didn't know how to register them all. It was overwhelming. I had scratches everywhere that felt like 1,000 little cuts from the thorny bushes I tried to escape through once I realized what he was about to do. My ankle was throbbing where he grabbed me to drag me out of those bushes. We wrestled, and he got me on the ground, and my arms felt like his hand marks would be permanently imprinted on them from the force that he threw me down with and then straddled me.

It was then that he got lucky- I kept fighting and trying to get up to push him off me, and each time he pushed me back to the ground. What he didn't know was that there was a rock just poking up from the ground, so each time he pushed me down, my head connected with the rock. I think it was the third time that I lost consciousness. When I came to, I felt I had gone through some horrible wormhole; I wasn't sure where I was or what was happening. There was nothing but confusion at first, and then the horrific scene came into focus as my vision gradually cleared. I felt the pain first and didn't understand it, as I had forgotten where I was and what had been happening.

As he stood over me, getting himself 'decent' again, he told me that I was not to tell anyone. I felt small, weak, and humiliated. He left me lying there on the ground, bashed, and beaten, half-naked, hurting, ashamed, scared, and confused as to whether this had all really happened or not.

After sobbing and weeping for I don't know how long because time was lost to my pain, I finally got myself covered and dressed. I tried to stand up to walk the rest of the way home. I immediately collapsed upon standing, unable to walk. Nothing was broken, but my body was saying, "we've been through enough, so, nope ... walking isn't going to be happening right now". So I started crying again, just longing for a safe place. Then, I started thinking, "Oh my god, what if he comes back?!?!"

This thought terrified me - I had to move - do something to get out of here ~ anywhere! Anywhere that was away from here. I figured any movement away from here and towards safety was a good move. So I willed myself to move. I was bargaining with my body, trying desperately to have it realize the urgency of the situation. I needed my body to see the importance of moving in this moment, now!

My body still stubbornly refused to let my legs work. In tears, my anger at my non-functioning, stupid body came rushing to the surface, where I decided legs or no legs, I'm getting the hell out of here. Who needs legs! I'll show you! So with non-responding legs, I crawled... I crawled with my arms and dragged my legs behind me. I crawled through the under-brush and through a field. I finally hit the fence that surrounded what was home, still terrified that he may be lurking behind me. I willed my legs to start working, as there was some climbing over the fence that was needed.

At first, they once again didn't want to cooperate, but after some tears and cajoling, shakily, I stood up and didn't really climb but more or less fell over the fence. After a flip falling over the fence, I finally managed to climb to my feet and walk home! I had left the party just before midnight for what should have been a 15-minute walk home. As I came into the house, I remember glancing at the kitchen clock. It was just after 3 AM, and all I thought was I had broken my 1 AM curfew.

I couldn't sleep, and the last thing I wanted to do was remove any clothing off my body. I wrapped myself in a blanket and rocked and cried, trying to process this horrific event. I felt so dirty and dirty on the inside, like I had been tainted right to my soul. I felt like I might not ever be clean again.

But I felt I needed to try because I couldn't take this dirty film on me – so I got into the tub and ran a bath, and with my clothes still on me, I sank down into the water. I don't remember how I got changed into dry clothes, but somehow, I did. I remember weeping in the tub. I felt so alone and that I must not ever let anyone know about this shameful thing that had happened. My illogical thoughts in those moments were that if I didn't talk about it or acknowledge it, it would just go away, and eventually, I could just dismiss it as a very bad dream... right?!?

For the next few months, my behavior changed drastically. I ended up breaking up with my boyfriend at the time since I would spend absolutely no time with him. I acted angry towards my father, and hugs or affection were absolutely spurned with such venom – I know I hurt and confused him.

I was angry over the ultimate loss of control, and, as I now see, I started trying to regain that control. I started working out three times a day. I controlled my diet with such strictness that I actually became concerningly underweight – gaunt was a word that was used often in my presence and the whispers.

My normally messy teenage room became spotlessly clean and organized to a military drill sergeant level. My school-work became an obsession for me – it afforded tons of ways to avoid boys and the whole high school social scene. I cut all my friends off, and my grades shot up, way up! My grade 11 average at that time was 97% in all my classes! I became obsessive about cleaning myself, finding any excuse to wash my hands and brush my teeth. I had showers a minimum of three times a day – short and quick ones because I didn't want to spend any time with my body. Especially my naked body.

My focus at first had great results: I became a parents and teacher's dream child, at first.

- my room was meticulously clean (any teenage parents dream)
- I became obsessive about schoolwork, which resulted in amazing grades
- I became obsessive about diet and exercise, which resulted in great weight loss, which was good at first

- I was cleaning myself constantly, which meant good hygiene

All good things, right???

But then my world, my secret, and my obsessions all came crashing in on me.

The vomiting started, which caused more weight loss, which was not what my already skeletal form needed. My parents rushed me to the emergency ward one morning as I had passed out cold.

Tests were done. Questions were asked. Food was offered as bulimia was the first thought.

I got scared, feeling defensive, desperately trying to grasp at keeping my secret still a secret. And after a day of a plethora of tests, the doctor walked into my hospital room looking at me with judgment in his eyes, and I somehow knew, he knows! Panic! He knew my secret... but how?

He asked my mother to leave the room, and I said she could stay. And with accusation in his voice, he asked if I was sure. I nodded yes. He then told me that I was pregnant. He spoke as if I should have been ashamed of myself. He told me with the attitude of "Why did you make us do all these tests if you already knew you were pregnant?" They had asked me if I was sexually active – to which I had answered no.

The rape had been my first time. And my only time up until then. I just couldn't acknowledge that technically I had had sex – that would completely destroy the castle of flimsy, filmy bubbles of protection I had built up. If I acknowledged that I had technically had sex, it would make the rape real for me, something I was not ready to do. But now, this doctor was treating me like a liar, and in my head, I was thinking, "He now thinks I'm a dirty lying whore." Was I? I did lie. So I was a liar and dirty, I was judgmentally rationalizing in my mind ~ these immediately were made my truths. Truths that would take years to excavate.

In a way, it was a blessing that mom was in the room – how could I have told her myself? I don't think I could have. I would have most likely done some desperate thing of "hoping it away." The nightmare continued, the bubbles were burst, the castle was burning, and I felt like there was no way out. I was on a forced march to devastation! Help!

Because my parents were extremely religious and even more pro-life, I became the poster child among their devoted pro-life warriors for why you don't ever get an abortion even after a rape! Many have asked me if I had had the choice, would I have had an abortion, and my answer and this my truth is, that it doesn't matter. Whether I would have or wouldn't have - I had to face this pregnancy to get myself through it. I am who I am today because of what I have had to face, to deal with, and get myself through. And, I love who I am today, and I wouldn't be me if I hadn't done that. It was part of my divine journey. I now know.

Shortly after that, I got shipped off to Toronto to a home for unwed mothers run by very sweet, well-meaning nuns. In reality, this home/school was a dumping ground for the pimps in the area and the strip club for the many strippers and prostitutes that found themselves pregnant by their johns... But that is an entirely different chapter. It gave me an education – not the kind of education my parents were envisioning, for sure.

But I made some great memories at that school – I met some very interesting, colorful, strange, amazing people. These were people who were living on a razor's edge. Theirs was a hard life, no nets, no plan Bs, no 5-year plans ~ in their world; one mistake can have them paying an extremely dear price. This time of my life often feels like another life altogether. Sometimes I wonder about the cast of this movie of mine; where are they now? Most are probably dead. They were friends for a season, a very weird, unusual season in my life.

I managed to get myself through the pregnancy. There were also some very tragic moments too. Moments that can't be unforgotten – these girls lived hard lives, and they often lived unforgiving lives too. I gave birth on May 16, just after midnight, after almost 20 hours of labor and after an emergency C-section, to two baby girl twins! My twins were not only healthy but the biggest twins on record for that hospital. Twin number one came in at 6 lbs. 9 oz., and my second baby girl was 8 lbs. 7 oz. That's a lot of baby! I knew I was going to be giving up these two beautiful girls. At that time, the policy was that you had to be outside of the hospital to relinquish your baby (or babies, in my case). So I was wheeled from the hospital in a wheelchair on the day of the discharge with one baby in each arm. Once I stepped into the parking lot, I handed my girls over.

It was the hardest decision I've ever had to make. But I know it was the right one for 17-year-old me at that time. Little did I know it would ultimately be an experience I could draw on time and again to make me an amazing counselor and, as I call myself, a Spiritual Sherpa. I needed to experience being totally, utterly, and completely lost ~ in order to later be a guide in the labyrinth of our shadows.

In the days and months that followed, I went into what I called "survival mode." I was in deep depression and unknowingly dancing at the edge of suicide. Every day I woke up, I would put a big red X on that day on my calendar, and the only goal for that day was to stay alive - to be here for the next day to make another big red X on the calendar. I felt as if I was in a nightmare that I couldn't wake up from. I couldn't think, I couldn't imagine, I couldn't dream or plan outside of the day. That day. Today. My focus was for today only.

I was alive. I just had to be alive today, this day, right now – I can die tomorrow. That was the deal; that was the pact I made with myself every single morning for months. I would say to myself, "I know you want to die, I know you want the pain to be over, I know you think there is no end to the hurting, But just stay for today. Stay alive for today, and you can die tomorrow." This is the promise I made to myself – you can die tomorrow. I didn't even have to live today – that was too much to ask – I just had to stay alive today. This was the deal I struck with myself every single day. I wasn't capable of living. I felt my heart and my soul had been ripped out of me. How was I supposed to live?!?! Let alone make plans?!

There are no plans outside of staying alive, and that was just a 24-hour pact. I made with myself every morning. I promised nothing after that.

But eventually, one day (and I don't remember the day), I decided I didn't need the red X on this day, and then I decided I didn't need my 24-hour agreement. I slowly started living past one day to two days, and then two days to three, and so on. It was a slow process, and honestly, I had almost forgotten how to live. But slowly, plans started being made. Smiles returned; sunny days were not only possible but now accepted. It was a long hard process. It was like climbing out of a thick muddy bog that I was into, up to my neck.

And why am I sharing my story? Well, for a couple of reasons…

I am constantly telling my clients no matter where you are, no matter where you've been, you are not doomed to a terrible life – you <u>can</u> get unstuck.

I can honestly say I know the edges of my life – I have been all too intimate with those edges. I am not just shooting my mouth off. I <u>know</u> how to come back to center. I know how to come back to living after surviving.

At the time when I presented the story, another reason became obvious for why I needed to share my story. We are each other's salvation, and we must witness each other's stories, especially with women. And when we listen without judgment to our sisters and allow space for a sister to express herself, what we are doing is we create a safe space for her to heal. We are actually activating a very ancient energy – for a spark of compassion and connection between our very souls.

In other words, when I tell my story, and other women tell their stories, and you witnessed me, and we witnessed them, we are unifying our feminine heart and sparking our healing energy, naturally and openly. We acknowledge our connectedness and allow others to join in the communal sigh of relief within the healing energy of the circle. Together we heal the wounded feminine essence; we strengthen the feminine soul.

Rhonda Devlin-Gilbert

EIGHT

THE INVISIBLE DISEASE

LIVING WITH FIBROMYALGIA

"Fibromyalgia may have changed my life, but I will change right along with it. I will create my life around the limitations I now face. I will fight the pain and I will fight the fatigue and I will become a better me because Fibromyalgia is not who I am, I am simply me." Fibromyalgia Helping Hands

I found myself a single mother at the age of 27 to four beautiful daughters. It's certainly not what I envisioned for my life, but here we were.

Life was fun! We were a thriving family who spent a lot of time outdoors going on wilderness adventures. We loved baseball, hiking, and swimming, and I had a great job that I loved. We were living our best lives.

I had a group of girlfriends, and we loved to go dancing at the local clubs every once in a while. I was certainly excited when we all decided we needed another girls' night out.

We decided to all meet at my home and go together from there. We were already in dance mode and were laughing and dancing with my daughters. We were having so much fun. It was then, in a single moment of time, that everything changed!

All of a sudden, I had excruciating pain! It terrified me, and I didn't know where it was from. Or what was causing it. My biceps and hamstring muscles felt like they were hard as rocks, and my body started to cease up. WHAT WAS HAPPENING TO ME?

I was flinging my arms up and down and marching high steps throughout the house to try and get these rock hard muscles to relax, trying to keep my cool around the girls, trying not to let them see me cry in excruciating pain. After about an hour, the pain was gone as fast as it started. I still decided to go dancing. Well, I tried to get all the thoughts out of my head and try to relax. Let me tell you that it did not work.

Omg, this was just a tiny taste of what was to come. The pain, muscle cramps, tightness, numbness, tingling, migraines, and memory loss. What was going on? The endless emergency room trips. The Doctor's appointments where I was trying to explain what I was feeling. This was just the beginning of the constant appointments, CT scans, MRIs, Bone Density tests, and blood work.

All the doctors would just give me new pain medicine as we tried to find something that would work. Some of the Doctors told me that this was all in my head. I even got thrown out of a Doctor's appointment as I couldn't walk as I was in such pain, and as I was hunched over the bed, the Doctor stated, "YOU ARE AN ADDICT LOOKING FOR MORE MEDS." Nothing was helping me.

I was literally going insane from the pain. Not being able to care for my children like I used to. I even forgot to pick up my children from school. That's when I started putting sticky notes everywhere. In the bathroom, kitchen, and yes, in my car to remember to pick up the kids from school. How does one live like this?

Thank goodness for the invention of the internet. Sitting on the computer for hours a day, putting in all my symptoms and just literally reading everything. Well, according to google, I had either Multiple Sclerosis or Fibromyalgia. So, I made an appointment to see my family doctor as soon as possible. Now I'm really freaking out. Who is going to care for my children? All the worst thoughts were running through my head. I can't focus. My head is so cloudy. I just wanted some answers.

As I was discussing my findings on what I thought I might have. The Doctor said, "he did not believe I had Multiple Sclerosis, but very possibly Fibromyalgia." My heart sunk deep in my chest as I sat and cried. I did my research and knew exactly what my life was going to be like now. He sent me for a neurologist appointment right away.

As I arrive at this appointment, my heart is pounding hard, and my body is so tight, like a huge rock. I almost feel like I'm going to have a heart attack. I can't sit to fill out the paperwork, hands shaking, having to pace the office as sitting was so difficult, and then having to bring the words I want to say to paper, but I can't remember how to spell my name.

After speaking to the neurologist, he did all of his testing and poked me in a pressure point (screaming and crying through each poke). The neurologist then said, "Tammie, you have Fibromyalgia. This is a neurological disease that attacks the nerves in your brain. They will never shut off and will short out all the time." I will never forget what he said to me. "I want you to know, Tammie, that this disease will not kill you, but it IS GOING TO MAKE YOUR LIFE A LIVING HELL. Also, I'm sorry, but unfortunately, there isn't much research or help for this, and here is another prescription to try."

All these meds I must take are not taking this awful pain away. Sleep helps a lot as you don't feel as much pain when sleeping. Here I was sleeping from the time my children went to school until they got home. I would manage to get homework done, then go back to bed. I would go until the next day. I certainly thank my lucky stars my mom was able to come and stay with me to help. She was the only one who believed me. She was my rock. All my siblings and nieces and nephews, cousins, and so-called friends thought I was just a drug addict. How can somebody sleep as much as her? She must be going through withdrawal.

Before I became ill with a chronic illness, I was there for everyone in my life. Now, I am sick. I look around and wonder, "Where are all the people, I was good to?" "Where did you all go?" This was the most challenging time of my life, and nobody was there for me besides my mom.

One day as I was doing little things around the house as much as I could. One of my sisters stops by. She asked me, "What the hell is going on with you? Do you remember going to Auntie Anne's funeral?" When did I go to a funeral?

With the shock in her eyes and her voice changed, I could tell this was something serious. It was then that I shared with her about my condition. She said, "Get all of your meds together and make a Doctor's appointment and get them all under control." Now I certainly understood and heard her when she said, "If you don't get this all figured out, I will call child services on you." That certainly opened my eyes as wide as they could go. She came with me to the Doctors and managed to get all my medication under control. I think I'm on the right path now.

After living with this for three years now, I was referred to the pain clinic at the local hospital, where I was getting local freezing injected into wherever I was having pain. Most times trying to make sure the most painful areas got it as there was only enough to do ten places. I was in the pain clinic every week as I was only getting two days of relief if I was lucky.

My regular Doctor I saw at the pain clinic was unavailable on one appointment, so I'm seeing a new person. Great, now I must explain everything again and again. I certainly was not looking forward to this. In walks a female nurse practitioner, I could tell she was listening to what I was saying as we talked. Ruth got me. She listened and wanted me to be better.

We discussed the current procedure and how many days of relief I would get. That was when she asked if I would be willing to try something different that she thought might help me. I said, "Sure, let's do it." Well, let me tell you that Ruth really changed my life. Adding something different made my two pain-free days to months at a time of being not completely pain-free, but I could go four months now with relief. Are you kidding me? I can walk, climb the stairs, drive my car, and take care of my children. These things I will never take for granted again.

After a few more appointments with Ruth, I decided I would only see her now. Now we were going to figure out how and why I ended up with Fibromyalgia. I have had surgeries every year since I was 15. Two major car accidents (jaws of life) were needed. These were neither my fault. Four births, with one being a C-section. And a lot of physical and emotional abuse for a small girl growing up. After a significant mental break down my father suddenly died of a heart attack in one of my sisters' backyards. All these things are significant factors in Fibromyalgia. Stress is the biggest factor for your nerves in the brain to short out and cause these flare-ups.

Learning how to manage the stress in my life was a big learning curve. I even took the courses that the hospital would offer to learn how to live with this and pain management. I had another baby and was able to manage the pain differently now. My life has never been the same since that night. I was meant to take a different path, and now I'm just walking my path my way.

It has only taken my family 18 years to believe that I'm not a drug addict. With another family member being diagnosed with the same condition, all eyes opened, and they finally believed me. Even with it being that long, I will take it!

I am now able to enjoy my life a little bit differently with my children and my grandchildren. I may not be able to keep up with them; they can certainly keep up with me.

If you are experiencing similar issues with your health as I have been, don't give up. Keep trying new things and talking to different medical people. You may find your blessed Ruth and it will change your life, as she did mine.

Tammie Trites

NINE

DRIP LOVE

A MOTHER'S JOURNEY THROUGH PARENTAL ALIENATION

"You will continue to suffer if you have an emotional reaction
to everything that is said to you. True
power is sitting back and observing everything with logic. If
words control you that means everyone
else can control you. Breathe and allow things to pass." -
Bruce Lee

I could not believe what I had just heard. And neither could Your Honor. My ex-husband's lawyer had just referred to me in court as "the other mother". The judge admonished him, but the feelings of that moment stayed with me for years.

You see, I knew at that moment that I was at war. Not just with my ex but with the entire system we call Family Law. This person knew nothing about me other than what my ex had told him. And here he was trying to diminish my role as a mother. He was trying to justify why he believed my ex's new wife should replace me. It wasn't an attempt to have all the adults in my daughter's life work together in her best interest. It was an attack on my character meant to wear me down and have me give up on my child. The comment made me furious in a way that you would imagine a mama bear feels when someone is threatening her cub's safety, and that feeling would revisit me many times over the following years.

Early on in our child custody case, I had come to accept that the man I was divorcing was no longer the man I married. He had made this very clear from the moment he told me he was walking away from our twenty-year marriage. I still remember how it felt the morning he asked if he could come with me for my usual walk. His request seemed odd as he hadn't ever asked before, even over the last month as I watched my Dad be ravaged by Parkinsons Disease and then pass away not two weeks earlier. As I heard the words "I want to re-invent myself," I felt nothing. I now know that my lack of response was shock, protecting me from lashing out at the coward in front of me. Twenty years of 'us' done. Over. Finite.

After that conversation and its timing, I guess I shouldn't have been surprised by the kind of lawyer I would be up against. A little-known fact is that Family Law practitioners are supposed to adhere to certain standards that are different from criminal lawyers, most likely because divorce is not a crime. Having said that, I was up against a lawyer who tried to make me feel like I was a defendant rather than a parent trying to put her child's needs before my own.

In hindsight, I wish I had retained a lawyer right away. But I believed that we could figure things out without the expense and nastiness of courtrooms. What an idiot I was. I did speak to a lawyer at one point, and I was disgusted by his "plan of attack". He clearly stated that I should keep my daughter away from her dad until I got whatever was on my wish list. I remember saying, "So you want me to use my daughter as a pawn?" and he replied, "That's one way to look at it." I didn't need my full half hour complimentary consult with this ass to know that we weren't a good fit.

In the beginning months of our separation, there was no written agreement for anything. My ex was not taking our daughter on a regular basis. He was not paying child support, spousal support, mortgage, business debt...nothing. So I was left a forty-six-year-old woman with a three-year-old child, and my recently widowed Mother lived with me. When friends asked me if I was going to start dating, I would think, "Oh sure. I'm such a catch with all that baggage!" I was angry at my ex's timing and lack of financial or emotional support for his daughter, but I knew I would muddle through. I always did.

So I began muddling. I could not afford a lawyer, so I researched the government websites and reached out to anyone I could that would help me navigate the system. I learned to file and respond to applications, address the judges, present evidence, the ins and outs of the Family Law Act, and the effects of high conflict divorce on children. But the fact was: I was not a lawyer. I read through The Family Law Act and court rules, which covered the basics of law. Unfortunately, none of that could prepare me for the attack of a lawyer who knew how to use the system to squash applications on technicalities, which would lead to me having to start from scratch.

There was, however, some humor to be found in the Halls of Justice. Like the day I found out I was still, I was legally married to my 'ex'. While trying to avoid having my ex pay any spousal support, the blowhard lawyer tried pointing out how I had made an error. I won't go into the lengthy explanation, but I didn't file for spousal support within the legal timeframe. He then made mention of another application that had not been dealt with within the legal timeframe, thinking that was also my error. But my paperwork told a different story.

It seems that my husband's first lawyer did not file a response to my original application, which made the entire application null and void...a fact that had been missed by the well-educated lawyers for eight years. Because our divorce had been granted on a void application, it didn't count. This did not sit well with my ex or his new wife (Yes, I'm laughing hysterically). Nor did they appreciate my mention of how the two wives were now "Sister Wives," according to the latest Reality TV show.

So, while I was doing everything in my power to keep my young daughter away from the adult issues that had such an impact on her life, my ex was hiring high-priced lawyers and preparing to give them more money than he would ever pay in child support. It was so very sad, but his actions made me believe that he hated me more than he loved our daughter, and by the time my ex was on his second lawyer, I felt things going from bad to worse.

The most painful part of the situation was watching what it was doing to my child. Research shows that children who hear constant, negative messaging about their parents feel that they are also being attacked. It is described as feeling that half of themselves are not good enough and not worthy of being loved. I began noticing changes in my daughter's behaviors. She was exhibiting signs of anxiety, especially after 3 or 4 nights of being away with her Dad. She was complaining about stomach issues and headaches. She would settle down after being home for a night or two...just in time to go back to her Dad's and cycle through the emotions again.

As she turned the corner to her twelfth birthday, she began actively trying to pit her dad and me against each other and was now loyal only to her Dad. She blamed me for everything wrong in her world. She began referring to me by my first name, telling me that was how her Dad and his wife referred to me.

When she was away, she would phone me and begin berating me, and when she was home, she would throw tantrums that would make a four-year-old proud, screaming how I was a bad parent. She managed to cover all the bases, such as telling me that I cared more about men than her and that I was making her Dad poor by spending the child support (he wasn't paying) on myself. I quickly realized that the words coming from her mouth couldn't possibly have come from her head or heart. At one point, she acknowledged that she talked to her Dad about our adult stuff, defending his actions by saying, "At least he tells me the truth!"

She also began avoiding any contact with her Grandma (my Mom), her older sisters, and the rest of our family. What I was witnessing was sickening and heart breaking.

It was about then that I began researching her behaviors and how she might be affected by what had become a high conflict divorce, whether I wanted it or not. Two words summed it all up. Parental Alienation. Or to those of us who have a more personal relationship with it, PA.

PA is a form of emotional abuse that arises almost exclusively in the context of child-custody disputes. For lack of a better word, it is a disorder in which children are programmed by an alienating parent. They embark upon a campaign of character assassination of the targeted parent. The children exhibit little if any ambivalence over their hatred, and it often spreads to the extended family of the targeted parent.

The belief of numerous child development specialists worldwide is that the most psychologically damaging thing that a parent can do to their child is to speak negatively or tell the child a lie about the other parent. Think about this: Every time you say something negative to a child about their parent, you say something negative about a part of them. And you are eroding the belief system that has been part of them since birth.

When a child is born, each parent forms a bond or attachment to the child. If this bond is based on the parent's emotional needs and not those of the child, the parent/child relationship is reversed from the beginning. When the separation between parents begins, that parent is more likely to put more pressure than usual on the child to support him or her emotionally. Because the child has spent their life trying to meet the parent's emotional needs, the child can often find this situation stressful and traumatizing. In an attempt at pleasing the parent and 'earning' their love, the child can be unable to resist the alienator's emotional need to disparage the other parent.

The child is placed in the position of being an emotional caretaker

Many parents often turn to their child during separation or divorce for emotional support. This does not alone make them alienators. We say things we later regret. We apologize to the child, take control and go back to being a parent. We make sure our child's emotional needs are met and then ensure ours are met by appropriately seeking emotional support elsewhere through a counselor, family, or friends. A good parent may make mistakes, but they own them. That's the difference between alienating your child and putting their best interests first.

Some alienating parents use money as their weapon to belittle the targeted parent and buy the child's devotion. This can be done when the alienating parent discusses adult subjects such as child support with the child.

If a parent physically abuses a child, doctors, police, and social workers will speak up and protect the child. But suppose a parent emotionally abuses a child. In that case, there is a greater likelihood they will get away with it because our court systems allow the parent to emotionally abuse their child unless the other parent can prove the damage done to the child in court.

At one time, PA was recognized by The World Health Organization as 'Domestic Abuse'. Unfortunately, before our legal systems had a chance to catch up to that notion, lawyers argued that PA was a legal term, not a medical term. Therefore a person had to seek a medical opinion from a professional in order to bring the accusation to court and be decided by a judge (who may or may not agree with the report). This action did nothing but make it more difficult for parents to protect their children from the emotional abuse of PA as it is a very costly endeavor. The only other option is to apply for a Sec 211 report, an extremely lengthy, invasive, and expensive procedure. Neither of these is a viable option for the average single parent relying on food banks and thrift stores to make ends meet.

In my experience, I was forced to defend myself in court and to my child as to why I had so many jobs during a two-year period. My child had been told I couldn't hold a job when in fact, I had 2-3 jobs at a time. Pre my divorce, I had been a Foster parent and employed in the Real Estate industry. I also volunteered in the community, and I'm not tooting my own horn, but I was not lazy. Post divorce, I had to arrange my employment around my special needs daughter, and I had to pay for child care as my ex would not contribute. I took any extra job that I could get, including retail, selling funerals, and cleaning other people's toilets.

One day my child came home and snidely said, "You can't hold a job, and you took all Dad's money" She was eight years old when these comments began. Eight years old. I still find it difficult to think back to those moments. I would have to try and explain the truth as I saw it, without mentioning that I thought her dad was an ass for damaging her heart in that manner.

Another issue that was used as a weapon against me was my living situation. As someone who had been left without any financial support and with a huge amount of business debt that had been incurred by refinancing our home, I had to claim bankruptcy. The house was sold, and I had to find suitable rental housing. In the first four years following the big "D", I moved six times. Each move was made carefully, and with my daughter's education being a deciding factor.

Due to her learning challenges (she was diagnosed with Dyslexia in grade two), I sought out school programs that would address her learning needs. My ex's take was that the moves were disruptive to our daughter. Thankfully the judge agreed that considering her special needs and the lack of support I was receiving; the moves were justified. But even with that, I was left feeling hopeless. Why did I have to defend myself against people who knew nothing about my child or me? Why did I have to defend myself because my ex hated me?

And why did my daughter, at 11 years old, tell me, "You just use men to pay your rent?" I realize that some readers can not imagine having their child say these things to them or anyone else for that matter. After parenting about two dozen children over the years, I have to say that I found the comments shocking. Once the shock passed, I found them disturbing and then heartbreaking. Not because I thought she believed what she was saying but rather because I knew she was being brainwashed, and there was not a damn thing I could do about it.

You see, when the child begins to mimic the alienating parent's hatred towards the targeted parent, the alienation is occurring. Ultimately, the child believes the alienator's viewpoint because, in order to provide support to this parent, he or she must do so. The choice for the child to not emotionally support this parent is not an option.

Parental alienation has occurred with the child as the weapon of destruction against the targeted parent. At some point, the child completely and wholly adopts the alienating parent's viewpoint about the targeted parent, and the cycle is complete. The child is without any empathy towards the targeted parent and sees them only as the alienating parent portrays them.

That's what goes through the child's brain. Then there is what happens when a parent tries desperately to correct the situation through the courts, which can only be described as a shit show. It's messy and very difficult to clean up. In some cases, it's seemingly impossible to clean up.

An excellent example of the term 'shit show' would be when my ex and I had been directed by the courts to work with a Parenting Coordinator (PC). I had asked for this form of mediation for about five years. My ex refused until, well, he decided it was his idea. The only hitch was that we had to agree on the person, which meant I had to agree to someone of his choosing because he would not consider anyone I put forward. I didn't care who it was because I understood that the PC was to act impartially and put our child's needs first and foremost.

We had a contract that laid out all the rules. I mean, what could possibly go wrong? Well, let me tell you. It took over a month to get the PC on board. She was so busy doing real lawyer stuff and changing law firms and decorating her new office that she didn't have the time to even meet with us, let alone put an action plan in place. Finally, two months after the $3,500 retainer had been paid, I had an appointment to meet the PC face to face.

As I settled into the styling office with the plush sofa, listening to the PC talk about herself, I couldn't help but think, "When are we going to start talking about my child?" So I politely directed the conversation by asking, "How are we going to help my child?" to which she said, "How do you think we can help her?" While thinking in my head, "I thought I was paying you thousands of dollars to help me, help her". I gave her some background on our situation, which included well-documented information on how my ex was systematically trying to alienate our child against me.

After I explained my version of events, the PC shared a little story with me. It went like this: "I had a client who was in your shoes. One day she came to realize that she just had to walk away from her kid. The emotional pain was just too much for both of them." It was a good thing I was already sitting down because my head fogged. I felt like vomiting all over her brand-new engineered wood floor. Was this person really telling me that as a Parenting Co-ordinator, she recommended I give up on my child?!

What the hell sort of person was I dealing with? Did she not hear me when I told her about raising not only my own three daughters but over two dozen Foster kids? Did she not hear me when I told her that I was raising my youngest, who has special needs and had been advocating for her mental health and education needs since birth? Did she not hear a word I said? I didn't want to hear someone say, "You may have to walk away." I wanted to hear someone say, "Let's all work together so that hopefully your daughter can have a healthy relationship with both her parents." As I left her office, I felt a cloud of doom forming over me. I felt my heart break.

If I'm, to be honest, I would have to say that there were a few extremely dark moments over the year following that meeting.

Times that I could not fathom how I would survive the hatred my ex was imposing on me by using our daughter as a weapon. Early on, I felt that the PC was also working against me, and I knew I must have sounded insane to some when I voiced my concerns because, quite frankly, my situation sounded like an episode of The Twilight Zone. My emails would go unanswered. I was not able to have much contact with my daughter as her dad was not cooperating with the custody agreement. I couldn't take him to court because we had to work with the PC to find solutions. But the PC was not answering my emails...it was a vicious circle.

At the same time, my daughter's head was being filled with lies about what type of parent I was, and though I knew in my heart she did not believe it, I struggled with watching her cross to the dark side so that she could prove her loyalty to her dad. During the few times I did see her, she was so full of anger and disdain for me. She became violent, and on more than one occasion, the police were called. To see your child handcuffed for her own safety and for yours, to see your child in a hospital bed on the psych ward, to have them bruise you and call you unimaginable names, to have them say, "Fuck off! I want my Dad." The worst memories I had of my daughter, and they were with me every single day. I honestly thought I was losing my mind.

One of the lowest points was when my ex refused to let me see my daughter over the Christmas holidays. By the time we finally scheduled an appointment a few days after Christmas, I had lost faith in the process. I remember feeling so many emotions as I drove the hour to Vancouver. I sat in the hallway outside the PC's office and listened to the wall clock tick. Five minutes. Ten minutes. Finally, the PC came out, looking surprised to see me, and said, "Why are you here?" My heart dropped as I asked where my daughter was?

The PC explained somewhat apologetically that my ex had canceled the appointment. My blood pressure blew a gasket, and any chance of me handling the moment with grace was not happening. I had messaged him twice the previous day about the appointment, and he had decided not to tell me he had canceled it. As I explained this to the PC, the tears of frustration flooded me. I wanted to drown in them, right there in front of her. I wanted her to see the damage she was helping perpetuate by not doing her f-ing job. Instead, I left the building in tears. I sat in my car, not able to wrap my head around what had just happened. I called my husband, who offered to come pick me up as he knew I shouldn't be driving. I promised him I would give it some time and have something to eat before I drove home. Then I turned up my radio and sobbed until there were no tears left.

The next couple of weeks were spent with me trying to get out of the parenting agreement so that I could make an application to the courts. This process left me feeling like I was a caged hamster on a wheel. I contacted the child welfare office (MCFD) and explained that my ex was keeping my child from seeing me. I was told that there was nothing they could do as it was a Family law issue, and I needed to contact either the police or the courts. I explained the situation and why I felt his actions fell under child abuse. This man was not only breaking the law by blocking access to my child, but he was blocking my child's access to her parent.

Under numerous sections of the Child, Family, and Community Services Act, his actions were considered emotional abuse of a child. This is the Act of which social workers turn to in order to determine if a child is at risk. I reminded them that it was their duty to follow up on any concerns brought forward with regards to a child's protection against abuse. By the end of the conversation, I was assured that someone would look into it. I was also told it could take several days as this was not an emergency situation. So I waited.

Ten days later, I was called back. The assigned worker had spoken to both my ex and my daughter. My ex told the worker that my daughter didn't want to see me, and my daughter said she felt safe with her Dad and they should tell me to f-off. The worker admitted having concerns but said there was nothing they could do because of my daughter's age (she was now 12 years old).

I was offered counseling services to help me cope and told my file would remain open in case I needed any other services. The thought running through my head was, "I don't need fucking services. I need my daughter". As I slowly wrapped my head around the fact that I might lose my daughter to the alienating behaviors of my ex, I became engulfed by depression. I woke every morning in sadness, and I cried in the bathtub each night.

To the outside world, things were "fine". My husband, friends, and family knew what I was going through and were my salvation. But all that was my normal had been brutally taken from me, and I didn't know how to get it back.

Then two things happened. The first came in the form of an email that I was never supposed to see. I'm guessing that in retaliation for my contacting MCFD, my ex arranged that a child protection complaint be made against me. I was not the least bit surprised when the social worker contacted me, nor was I surprised when it was dismissed as a non-issue. However, I was shocked to find out that it was made after my ex had a telephone conversation with our Parenting Co-ordinator by our Parenting Coordinator. Now, imagine my anger. No, try again. IMAGINE MY ANGER.

The professional I had paid to act as a neutral party and protect my child's best interests had acted on a complaint from a man who hated me. She did not ask me for clarification. She did not even consider he might be making shit up. She just picked up the phone and tried to break me once and for all by asking the child welfare folks to take my daughter from my care. She then had an email conversation with my ex, who was thanking her for acting so quickly on his complaint. It was an absolute conflict of interest and one that I actually got an invoice for. Seriously, that is how stupid some people are.

I am of the belief that as long as lawyers can make obscene amounts of money and are not called on their stupidity, evil will happen at their hands. I took action against our PC, which included a complaint to the Law Society, and then I rested. I decided that the entire court process was working against my child and decided to spend my energy on finding a way to bring her world back to some form of normal.

The second thing was what I think of as the most significant message my angels sent me. I came upon an article about Parental Alienation written by a woman who talked about how she chose to let love heal her relationship with her child. And love won. She would text her child every few days just to say hi. No expectations of a reply. Just a drip of love. It took a few months, but eventually, she got a "Hi" back. From there, the healing began.

I have to be honest. I had no intention of waiting months for results. I was beginning to suffer from blood pressure and stress ailments. I knew the cause was my broken heart, and I wasn't sure how much longer I could go on. I figured that if this other woman (and many others I came to know) could find a way to rebuild their relationships with their children, I surely could. But I had to get to the root of the problem without alienating my daughter further.

So I began. I sent funny animal videos. I sent texts that said, "Was just thinking about and hoping you are having a great day" or "thought you might like to know that..." At first, I got responses like "Go away" or "STOP!" But I stayed strong. Drip. Drip. Drip. Then I got a "LOL" in response to a funny video. After another few days, I got a "Will you take me for sushi? But you can't tell Dad." My heart exploded with joy, and then I felt sadness. The joy was obviously from the hope of re-connection, but the sadness was because I could tell she was afraid of what her dad would say or do.

There were a few more months that put me back in the hamster cage at times, But I continued to drip love. There were moments I almost gave up, but I had made my daughter a promise long ago, and I'm not a promise breaker. I told her, "There is nothing you can do or say that would make me ever stop loving you." I knew what love meant to my daughter, which was if you love someone, you never give up on them. I will never forget the day she screamed at me, "You can't give up because you promised!" I didn't like the screaming, but I loved the message.

In a few days, my daughter will turn sixteen. There is so much more to this story. For now, I want you to know that when I hear her laughter, all the painful memories disappear. I watch her as she grows into an amazing human, slowly but surely. She is my daughter, and no lawyer, no government body, and no hateful others could tear us apart. And for that, I am grateful.

B'elle Meraki

PITY PARTY OR CHAMPAGNE?

WHEN DEATH KNOCKS ON YOUR DOOR, HOW WILL YOU ANSWER?

"Life should not be a journey to the grave with the intention of arriving safely in a pretty and well preserved body, but rather to skid in broadside in a cloud of smoke, thoroughly used up, totally worn out, and loudly proclaiming, 'Wow! What a Ride!"
- Hunter S Thompson.

The bright sun beaming down interspersed with a soft, gentle breeze. Laughter in the background as our family gathered for a summer bbq – when out of the blue, a wet – sucking noise interrupted so rudely! Reality set in; IT was in our space, my mother in IT'S grasp.

August 2019 (Pre-COVID) I was nearing the end of my recovery from a partial hysterectomy to help rid the agonizing condition of Endometriosis. Grateful that my parents, who had just arrived in April 2019 to live beside us, were close by to help when my husband was away for work.

Early September 2019, Life was feeling really good! Life had a nice rhythm to it, an easy ebb and flow. Out of the blue, so it seemed, my mother wound up in the ER with abdominal pain, and this was a rare occurrence! My mom had a pain threshold like no other, so for her to complain really meant that something was 'off'. This was a Thursday, and in the blink of an eye, life's rhythm was interrupted.

After completing a few tests, it was discovered that mom's bladder was the size of a football. A blockage somewhere along the line was creating a backup – hence the discomfort. The ER staff drained the excess fluid and sent her home with directions to return for follow-up and further testing in the morning. Further testing quickly revealed the 'C' word, Cancer, Ovarian Cancer to be exact. The blockage was a large tumor that needed to be removed ASAP. IT – Cancer had arrived to disrupt the ebb and flow of life around us.

Much like Santa calling for his reindeer, On Donner, On Blitzen, it seemed like a team was assembled in the blink of an eye, and a plan was put in place stat! My mother came home on Friday, heavy with all the information, and shared the news with my dad by her side. Shock, disbelief, why me, why her? All of the stuff rushed up to the surface.

My mother was already a Breast Cancer survivor and had been Cancer free for about 11 years. A partial hysterectomy after having children (me and my brother) really left us with a ton of questions – but there was no time for that! She had a bag to pack, pack, sit and wait. My mother had been put on an emergency surgery list, and if an OR (operating room) became available during the weekend, she would be called and given just a moment's notice to prepare and arrive for surgery.

The call came Saturday morning to head in to be prepped. Off she went, bag in tow and my dad by her side. Prepped for surgery, she and her team waited – bumped – a more pressing case came in, and my mom was sent home with a plan to return Monday morning. She would be the first one in. Bumped? This was great news! For us, it meant that if someone else's case was more pressing, then my mom was in pretty good form!

Monday morning came and off Mom and Dad went again. The surgery was scheduled for a couple of hours, and then my Dad would call with an update. We already knew my mom was going to be in the hospital for a couple of nights to recover. A couple of hours go by, a few pass by, nothing! No word! Calling my Dad, he had no updates either, and I could hear the worry in his voice.

Finally, an update came. The tumor was greater than expected, and another surgeon was called in to assist. The tumor had dipped into the bowels and was also across the diaphragm. They were not prepared for what they saw. The surgical team was able to avoid a colostomy bag but could not guarantee that this had been avoided for good. If the healing did not go as planned, this option was still on the table, and my mother was adamant that a colostomy bag was not an option for her!

Mom's leading Doctor gave a lot of information, and it was a lot to take in and digest. He was confident that he had gotten all of IT -the cancer - but the naked eye could only see so much. Chemo. It was next on the agenda, and it would be an aggressive round based on the mass and spread that was found. The Doctor had hope and gave hope; we were confident that things were on the upswing. After all, you can't keep a Good Girl down, and my mom is a fighter!

My mom's body decided to extend her hospital stay into a 'staycation'. Blood would not clot, so transfusions were required, antibiotics thru IV for an infection, and the list goes on. When you are active and like to be on the go, your body quickly takes control and does what is necessary to keep you in check. Oh boy, oh boy, was my mother in check! A couple of days turned into a couple of weeks, and finally, my mother was granted freedom to come home. Well, freedom, so to speak. Daily visits were now part of my mom's 'regular' routine. PSW's (Personal Support Care Workers) for wound care, nurses for vital checks, etc. It seemed to be a revolving door, but at least the door was attached to their home and not her hospital room.

Recovery was underway, and spirits were high! A PICC line was now 'installed' into my mom's left arm, creating ease for bloodwork and preparing for chemo. The nurse flushed it regularly to keep it clean and prevent infection.

During one of the regular nurse visits, a slight fever was detected, indicating an infection somewhere in the body, and just like that, my mom was back in the ER to be checked. Tests revealed an infection in her blood, and another 'staycation' was booked as she was admitted for IV antibiotics and careful monitoring as this infection could be deadly. Not 100% certain of the cause, it was believed that the picc line could have been the cause, and it was removed from the arm and later replaced embedded in her chest.

Thanksgiving 2019 (October), and the sun was shining on the back deck. A cool fall breeze danced over our faces, and children laughing were all present – the only thing missing was my mom as she was confined to her hospital room. IT was present even though we didn't fully realize how present IT was.

Home and recuperating chemo started in November 2019. This necessary life interruption would become the new routine. Every 3rd Tuesday, my mom went for bloodwork to check her system to see if her body was well enough to receive the treatment. Every 3rd Wednesday, my mom went for chemo treatments lasting six hours. Life interrupting this was, but Life Saving was the plan, and interruptions were welcome as it meant that she was still here fighting, fighting hard with an attitude of gratitude. Yes, there was fear, tears, and exhaustion, but there was laughter, there were hugs, there was life – life worth living.

As my mother entered into chemo, I underwent another round of surgery to complete a full hysterectomy – I was not taking any chances and my birthing years were long over. What I was not prepared for was the other conversation that my Gynecologist had with me.

My mom had had Breast Cancer and now Ovarian Cancer – there was a strong possibility that she could be a carrier of the BRCA Gene, and if this was the case, I had to consider what my options were. If my mom were BRCA positive, it would be suggested that I (and my daughter) consider a double mastectomy as a preventive measure to ward off Cancer. In this moment, my world got fuzzy, my brain swirled, and my breath became shallow. "Not to be vain," I said, "but I quite like these" (motioning to the breast area on my body) "unless you are putting something back on – these are not coming off!" Sucker punched in the moment we moved on to the matter at hand and discussed the upcoming surgery.

My mom had been given the option of participating in a trial program. This would mean that she would get her chemo but would then go on to additional treatments. The additional treatment phase would be an unknown as a trial is a blind test. Some candidates get a placebo, and some get the test drug. The trial program also meant advanced monitoring and testing, and for this reason, my mom was all in! The downside was life would continue to be interrupted every three weeks – 3rd Tuesday bloodwork, 3rd Wednesday treatment, and in between CAT Scans to monitor the inside. Testing for the BRCA Gene came back NEGATIVE (PHEW!!!!!).

February 2020, we gathered for mom's last round of chemo. My dad, my daughter, and her son, and I sat by and waited. And then we walked over to the wall where the bell was mounted, and my mom rang the bell. She rang it loud and proud to signal that the Chemo Phase had ended, and she was still living with an attitude of gratitude. Not everyone makes it through the Chemo Phase, so to ring the bell is an emotional moment to acknowledge the strength, will, and opportunity to be present in everyday life. Now the trial phase would begin.

As the world came to a screeching halt with the unleashing of a global pandemic COVID 19 – my mom, like the trooper, she is carried on with her treatment. Only now, it looked different. She had to go in alone as my dad waited out in the car for her. Regular Doctor visits with her Cancer Doctor and team were done solo – no one was allowed to accompany her – my dad would patiently wait in the car, and like clockwork, my mom would emerge with a smile on her face until...

Until May 2021. The world still in the throes of COVID and our local communities doing the best they could to navigate the circumstances at hand. Sadly, in the blink of an eye, we would see first-hand how these challenging times would shed light on a system in need of repair.

My mom arrived for her usual check-up. Expecting nothing but the norm that she had become accustomed to. After all, this strong, magnificent woman had been undergoing treatment since September 2019 with her 1st surgery, and every three weeks since November 2019, she was poked and prodded. Her body was treated for a disease we could not see – IT was ever present, silent but intrusive all at the same time.

Imagine being alone in a room with a team of Doctor's as you were told that the latest CAT scan showed the return of another tumor. The diagnosis was harsh. There are two kinds of Ovarian Cancer, and one is very aggressive with no cure... YES! You guessed it. My mom had the aggressive, no cure kind. Crying and alone in a room full of Doctor's, my dad, who was waiting in the parking lot, was called, and he was put on speaker. He could hear his loving wife of 52 years crying in the background while the Doctor's shared the news with him. He could not reach out and offer a hug of support. He could not cry along-side her – both of them alone doing the best they could to grasp the gravity of the news. My mom stumbled out to the car, and homeward bound they went.

I will never forget the moment they arrived home. The sing-song voice was vacant as my mom shared the news with tears streaming down her face. "Why me?" "What have I done to deserve this?" "What will your father do?" All the big questions bubbled to the surface and just rolled off her tongue –

you could feel the sting of each question, the gravity of the situation – IT – the Cancer yet again stealing the limelight from this vibrant woman. How dare IT interrupt our life! How dare IT shatter our ebb and flow! How dare IT think that my mother was up for grabs!!!!!

The next few days are a blur, you can never see clearly through the haze of tears, and the tears did flow. Trying to come to grips, my mother attempted to make plans. "Well," she said, "We will need to put your dad on e-harmony! He is too young to be by himself!" Just like that, my mom was 'looking' after everyone else's best interest...we quickly put the kibosh on that! We rallied together and had a serious conversation to set the record straight.

You see, the Doctor's informed my mom that they were in it to win it as long as they could. No, they did not have a timeline – they knew she had more than just mere days or weeks but could not promise months or years. What they did promise was that they would fight right along with her. To give her (and us) quality and quantity of life, and just like that, surgery was booked to remove the new tumor.

Surgery day arrived, and not only would they be removing the tumor, but they would also repair a hernia. The original surgery in September 2019 required a previous hernia repair to be released to access the bowels that needed to be removed. Due to the inner work needed at that time, the hernia had to be left as it was. This had left a huge bulge in my mother's abdomen, making it appear as if she had gained a significant amount of weight – the appearance waned on my mom's self-image as if losing all of your hair to chemo wasn't bad enough!

Two surgeons would be going in, one to remove the tumor and one to install a mesh lining and repair the hernia. The surgery went as expected, and another round of recovery began. This time it felt different. COVID had restrictions in place, and no visitors were allowed, my mom was alone in a hospital room to heal. The mental stress impacts the physical, and when she came home, she looked worn, pale, and her smile was a little dimmer – but home she was, and we were thankful that her feet were on this side of the earth.

The routine began all over again! Medical supplies being delivered for aftercare, PSW's and nurses coming and going and ahhhh YES, the glimmer in her eyes, the brightness of her skin and her smile began to appear again, vim and vigor were doing their best to overshadow IT. A short week later, my phone rang at an early hour – an ambulance was enroute for my mother – I quickly went next door, thankful that they were just at the end of my porch.

My mother had been getting sick all night and was not in good form – a belly full of staples and stitches on the inside and out, and each wretched heave brought up bile, pain, and the waning of hope. The paramedics arrived and whisked my mother away – at that moment, they were our knights in shining armor – kind, caring, and compassionate – she was in good hands. My dad re-packed her bag and followed behind to the hospital.

COVID, we were still under attack! Relentless, unkind, uncaring, and unforgiving COVID. My dad turned away – my mom alone - no overnight bag, no cell phone for family contact. Restrictions still in place, no backup plan for the mental health that goes along with the physical needs, doing the best they could but, but we were frustrated! The vomiting had been so intense that the stitching of the mesh had begun to break, and the mesh was now obstructing the bowels. Prepped again, my mom was back in the OR to repair the mesh lining; seriously, can a woman not get a break?

My dad waited in the car and heard back that all was okay – yet my mom was again, alone, beaten down, and scared. A few days later, home to recover. Each day home saw her spirits rise as her attitude of gratitude bolstered, and the sing-song voice had the melodic tune back in stride. We seemed to be over the hurdle!

Not so fast, my darling! A mere one week later, my mother went to the bathroom as her shirt was wet, trying to figure out what was happening. Her belly, between the staples, was gushing much like a pop bottle that had been shaken and released – back she went to the ER. Yet again, no entry for anyone else, my dad banished to the car to wait again. This visit was not so smooth. Nurses were overworked and under-staffed, meaning that my mother was treated to very little care, concern, or dignity. By now, she was broken, the fight leaving and the sharpness of her tongue was razor sharp, she had enough, just enough!

When the attending staff were able to see her, it was determined that an infection was present, and boom, just like that, another 'staycation' was booked. A new team rallied, working along-side her usual team of Doctor's. Infectious Control were brought in to investigate. And it was determined that my mother's body was rejecting the mesh and the infection was huge.

Antibiotics via IV, poking and prodding all the while alone. There was no support to help digest the information, the next steps, the squeeze of a hand, a loving hug – she alone to manage the best she could in trying times. The level of infection was too high for surgery at this time, the incision was opened and packed with sterile material to keep the wound closed, and a VAC Machine was inserted into her belly. VAC – vacuum assisted closure- VAC uses negative pressure (suction) to help bring the edges of your wound together. It also removes fluid and dead tissue from the wound area. A machine is used to do this. A special covering is put over the wound. Then a tube connects the covering to the machine. The machine creates the suction. The machine never leaves your side. It is carried like a purse, a black box with what seems like miles and miles of tubing – that wet sucking noise ever present in the background as the infection is drawn out and the wound closes over time. A gentle reminder, this is still just the month of May expanding into the first week of June 2021.

A little perplexed by this new addition of 'issues' my mom's teams rallied together to create a plan. Another full treatment plan for Chemo was still on the horizon, and another surgery was imminent to remove the mesh from inside her body. We were at a standstill. The infection needed to be minimized before anything else could move forward. Chemo compromises the immune system, and a system already under attack could not bear another slam.

So we waited, the wet sucking noise now a part of the day in and day out. The VAC grew heavier each day as my mom's shoulder bore the constant weight. The one good thing is that the VAC is portable, and a baggy sweater could hide the appearance a bit, giving my mother some dignity as she went about her daily activities.

June, July, the infection keeps paring down, the wet sucking noise still present but not as vocal. August saw the start of chemo once again. The fear was that if the chemo did not start, the tumor removal would be all for nothing. Every three weeks, the routine began again. Finally, Mid-August saw the wound healed enough, not entirely, but enough that my mother was released from the arms of the VAC, and the bruising on her shoulder could start to mend.

August 2021 was a good month! Chemo started, VAC removed, and finally, my brother who lives in the States could finally cross the border to visit. You see, just prior to COVID, my brother and his wife had a little girl, and during COVID, baby #2 came along. FaceTime allowed my parents to see their new grandchildren, but August 2021 found those grandchildren wrapped in their arms, hugged tight – something facetime just can't give you. My brother extended his stay and visited for two glorious weeks, but we all knew that good-byes would need to come at some point. IT silent, yet ever present. My brother squeezed my hairless (thanks to chemo) mother tight. No one wanted to say it. Would this be the last time he hugged her? The last time he felt her in his arms? They are questions that we don't have answers for, but hope, we do have hope.

My mother is strong, resilient, and living an attitude of gratitude. Grateful for each day, her feet are planted on this side of the earth. Some days are rough, days where the tears flow even when she does not want them. On these days, she grants herself permission, permission to have a Pity Party. Permission to sit with the tears, the anger, the why me? All of it! You see, when my mother shared her news just a few months ago in May, we knew some days would be downright tough! The only words of advice I could give my mother were: It is okay to have a Pity Party to sit in the mess and all the emotions but dear mother of mine, the next day rise and pop the Champagne because you have so much more living to do. It does not deserve to be the highlight – my mother's bright, beautiful smile, the melodic sing song voice, the spice for life, and zest for living that is to be celebrated.

I know this to be true watching my mother battle, an attitude of gratitude, the vim, and vigor of the will to live, and the mental fortitude and resiliency is 80% of the battle. Science and Doctors can work their magic, but if your will to live is not stronger than the science, then IT will surely win every time. Odds can be beaten, miracles can happen, and our family believes in hope and miracles. We have Faith and are ready to walk the path given to us. You can't keep a good woman down, and my mother stands loud and proud – here for a good time and a long time!

There is one thing I know for certain; Death will knock on each of our doors. It is a guarantee.

For all I know, I may very well transition out of this world before my mother. We can't see our expiry dates – yet we all have one. Unexpected and life-altering diagnoses occur each and every day. So, let me ask you, "When death knocks on your door, how will you answer?" Will you offer it a pity party and drift into the arms of despair, or will you POP the Champagne and live life to the fullest? For my mother, 80% of her days are POP the top and 20% Pity Party – pretty good odds, I say. If you can take away just one thing from my mother – live today for today! Show up with an attitude of gratitude and be thankful your feet are on this side of the grass.

As this goes to editing and print, my mother is halfway through her chemo. And once her body has healed from the surgery, the mesh removal still awaits her. Her hair has fallen out, and her abdomen protrudes from the hernia released. Her eyes sparkle, her laughter is infectious, and her sing-song voice is music to my ears. You can't keep a good woman down, and my Mama is pure evidence of that. When her time is called, the heavens will proclaim, "WOW! What a ride" as she slides in with a cloud of smoke, thoroughly used up and totally worn out. You have but one life to live...live it with an Attitude of Gratitude and make my Mama proud!

Sheri Godfrey

ELEVEN

FROM SCARCITY TO SIMPLY SPLENDID

A STORY OF TRANSFORMING STRUGGLE TO MANIFEST A LIFE OF ABUNDANCE AND GRACE.

"There is enough, I have enough, I am enough."
Leanne Giavedoni

"Even if I was the President of the United States, it still wouldn't feel like enough!"

I can remember the day I spoke those words out loud. I was standing in my treatment room speaking to my physiotherapy client. She expressed how inspired she was by my accomplishments and how proud I must be that I was an educated professional with two degrees, married to my high school sweetheart, with the million-dollar family and a brand-new clinic. She was genuinely complimenting me, but I didn't see what she saw. As she left, I found myself thinking about what I said, over and over. What was wrong with me?

Of course, all of that was true. And what people saw. But there was so much more I held close to my heart and didn't share with anyone - not even my family at times. So much pain and disappointment left me feeling empty and certainly not happy. I tried to cover the pain by doing, achieving, and being super-woman by always striving to be more and do more. But every goal I achieved didn't fill the void. I still felt like I wasn't good enough, and the path to my achievements was filled with so many hardships and struggles.

But I was good at ignoring the feelings, or so I thought. I ignored my problems by focusing on helping others with theirs. After all, I could do it in the name of my profession as a Physiotherapist.

By my thirties, the years of pain started to show up on my face and in my body. I looked worn out and barely smiled. I had shoulder pain, irritable bowel symptoms, allergies to every-thing, and PMS. My doctor said it was stress, until one day, when I broke down crying in his office, he changed his diag-nosis to depression and handed me a prescription for an anti-depressant. The diagnosis devastated me. I was also stubborn and refused to give in to his diagnosis and solution. After all, I was a drugless practitioner, and finding ways to heal the body without medication was my profession.

I set out on a mission to find answers to why I felt the way I did and how I could fix it. Little did I know where my search would take me. It is one of many twists and turns and lots of surprises.

Along my path, I had picked up the saying, "be prepared to be surprised". My Medical Intuitive teacher first said to me never assume the meaning of the impression you are getting. But for me, it holds more significant meaning and is applied to all areas of my life. You might think you understand something or that you have figured out how things need to be and then the surprise. You get what you want, but it looks nothing like what you thought it would be. Sometimes the realization is immediate, and other times it is after the fact and, in my case, even decades later.

I found myself visiting an alternative healer to have my "chakras balanced". I was skeptical, to say the least, but a very dear friend suggested it. Plus, I was starting yoga, and they always mentioned the third eye chakra, so I figured I would go and come back relaxed. I had no idea what it was all about, but I was desperate to feel better. That session was crazy! A childhood trauma that I had blocked out came to my awareness while lying on her treatment table. I was crying and yelling for it to stop, perspiring and struggling to break free. I learned later that it is possible to block out very traumatic experiences as a protective mechanism, but they still exist in your subconscious. It made so much sense and started to help me see why I had some of the fears and feelings I did.

I continued to have these treatments for a number of months, and more traumas were dealt with. I revisited some bullying that happened from grades four to eight, some rebellious behaviors I engaged in through my teens, and even the brutal murder of my older brother. Those were some intense sessions, but I felt some of the armor over my chest lift each time. I was feeling lighter, and people even commented on something looking different about my face.

As I was releasing the emotions connected to these memories, I noticed that I was becoming more and more intuitive - like I could do what my healer was doing for me. I was so pumped. I thought I could take on the world as these weights were lifted from me. I felt like I had stumbled on to an incredibly amazing way to help others have the transformation I had just experienced.

I felt so excited because I had a vision of helping others with their health and wellness for as long as I can remember. This felt like the missing piece. I can recall sitting around a table sharing the beginning of that vision with my siblings back in the late 1990s.

At the time, I envisioned owning a wellness center that had multiple health and wellness practitioners working together. It was a mix of traditional doctors, physiotherapists, chiropractors, massage therapists, social workers, naturopaths, and acupuncturists. Now with this experience, I would add alternative practitioners like Yoga instructors, Reiki healers, and even a Medical Intuitive. You might imagine this was a pretty unique vision for that time. At the time, people considered chiropractors, acupuncturists, and naturopaths "alternative medicine". Yoga was entering the dawn of its acceptance, and the rest was more in the realm of voodoo and charlatan. They did not belong in the same sentence as medicine at all. Today perhaps there are still some that hold the same view, but these options are certainly more widely known and explored by many as part of their wellness options.

In my vision, I also saw hairdressers and aestheticians as part of a wellness model because of the significance feeling beautiful plays on people's emotional well-being. Every year I would write out my vision for this team of like-minded health and wellness providers working together, yet all independently owning their part of the business. Each person had a common goal while managing and creating their own business with autonomy, individual flair, and specialty. I included details in my vision about the freedom and peace it would provide me while having a significant impact on people's wellness. I imagined the ripple effect of people feeling happier and healthier, making our world a better place.

The vision of it brought so much joy. But the reality of it was full of pain and suffering.

I attempted to bring this dream to fruition multiple times. Each attempt, I fell short of the vision. Each time I dug deeper into my pocket - each time making and losing friends along the way.

I was a hardworking Physiotherapist owning my own business with this relentless vision for how I saw health care providers coming together and a desire to see changes in the way people deal with health and wellness. This desire sent me on an exploration of all sorts of alternative approaches. Applying traditional, with alternative, with spiritual, with new age, with science was a regular everyday occurrence for me. I had a wealth of knowledge, and I shared it with and helped many people, but I could not make a penny doing so.

It made no sense. I had all the skills, all the tools, and the ability, but for some reason, money escaped me. I paid to share my services. Yes, you read that correctly. I earned zero pay for half of my career as a physiotherapist, and I went into debt multiple times to fund these businesses to the point I was advised I should declare bankruptcy. I resisted that and found ways to refinance my home but carried so much guilt that I had wasted my husband's hard-earned money on my failed business. How is that possible? What was wrong with me? What was I doing wrong? I thought I released all that stuff from my past, so why was I still struggling so much?

I felt like a masochist, punishing myself again and again. But I couldn't do it anymore, and I had to check out for a whole year. I didn't want to be who I was anymore, but I didn't know who I was otherwise.

After being diagnosed as depressed and my third business attempt failed, I needed to check out from this chapter of my life for a full year. I couldn't deal with anything more. The unraveling that was happening was exhausting. I do not know what felt worse, closing another business, losing tons of money, people deserting me, or not being able to handle the whole situation emotionally. I felt weak and stupid. Every day after the kids went to school, I went into a room I set up with an Ikea recliner and just sat there meditating, journaling, and reading self-help books. Sometimes I cried, sometimes I was angry, sometimes I would just fall asleep. Then when the kids got home, I would put myself together and be their mom.

But I had to put myself together, I had to go back to work, we needed to get out of debt, and it required two incomes. I found a couple of jobs working for others as a Physiotherapist, but after a year, I found myself drawn to that vision of the health and wellness model I had in my heart. I resisted the pull for as long as I could, but the vision would not die. Trust me, I wanted to run away from it and even tried, but it followed me like the plague. I longed to feel successful and see this vision to fruition and yet I was terrified of the possibility of failing again.

I was on my fourth attempt at pulling this vision off, and it was failing yet again. It is one year into my fourth clinic, and things are bad. My partners are gone, and I am alone. I am struggling to make ends meet, working my ass off, and getting more and more stressed. I am sad and angry. I can't believe I am here yet again, and there is no way in hell I am going into that depressed state I ended up in the last time. At my wit's end, lying in bed, looking up at the ceiling like I am talking to some universal power. I let it have it and give it a piece of my mind as I cry that I am tired of this crap. I am doing my part to serve and love, and it is about time things lighten up for me.

I am just ranting like people do when they are pissed, and I was pissed. I managed to doze off and get some sleep. In the morning, I did my routine, and when I was checking my emails, I saw something in my junk mail that caught my attention. Now you know that you get all kinds of junk emails, especially when you run a business, people message you lots. You and I both know you ignore them, delete them, and don't give them a second glance. But something captured my attention. After all, I did have a heart-to-heart last night with the universe. Maybe it was listening for a change. I messaged the lady and agreed to meet with her at my clinic to discuss a business opportunity that involved natural supplements.

To explain, I had used supplements and natural products to help get me out of my depression. It was part of my wellness routine, and I was clear that I wanted it to be part of the habit of those I was helping create a better lifestyle. I had been investigating brands I could sell at my clinic for almost two years, so I was excited to meet with this lady to learn about these supplements I saw in the picture, hoping this could be an answer.

This lovely lady came in with a small wooden box and some brochures. She opened the box and pulled out some brown bottles with liquid in them, and proceeded to tell me about essential oils. Now I have no clue what essential oils are, but I patiently wait for her to bring out the supplement bottles I saw in the picture. Nope. She proceeded to share with me about the business opportunity she mentioned in the email. She was probably too focused on her job to notice me looking up at the ceiling while having a conversation in my head. This is your answer to my plea? Essential what? And network marketing, what? Are you kidding me? Is this some joke?" But in my heart, I kept feeling I needed to hear her out.

Finally, I asked her where the supplement bottles were, and she was a little surprised but did direct me to the website where I could learn more. From a business perspective, the opportunity was very attractive, and there was nothing to lose. Personally, I had no clue if this stuff would work, and I did not want to waste money on it, and I definitely would not recommend it to my clients before trying it myself. So, I decided to give the products a try.

Although I had gotten out of my depressed state, I was still experiencing IBS and PMS. My son was also dealing with acne and digestive issues. The essential oils I chose for my concerns worked amazingly within three months. I was blown away! All those years of suffering, and I was finally having relief. I remember the day my husband told me that he was so happy to have his wife back - I still get tears in my eyes when I recall that moment. My son's issues took longer, but eventually, we mastered a protocol, and today you cannot tell that he had terrible acne. I couldn't help but wonder if my life might have been turning around?

Fast forward three years after meeting "the lady" who introduced me to the essential oils. My clinic failed, and I found myself closing down my business yet again. It took me a long time to accept that things can fail, yet you do not have to feel like a failure. This time, as I closed my doors for the fourth time, I did not feel like a failure. I was leaving this model of healthcare and this way of running a business, but my vision was still alive and well.

I would continue to empower people to make healthy lifestyle choices and teach them about taking care of their body, mind, and spirit. I would go on to work with a large team of like-minded individuals who are all working together for the same goal, independently contributing in their unique ways. Be prepared to be surprised; proved correct yet again. You never know how it will all come together, but if you keep going, it always finds a way to work out and often better than you could have imagined.

Probably the biggest surprise of all is the personal and spiritual growth I have encountered along the way. I am an intellect, and I love to delve into how the mind works, how life works, and how the universe works. Yes, I am one of those people that asks why the sky is blue. I have been on a conscious journey to make my life better since my early thirties. Before that, it just felt like life happened randomly.

Until my forties, the desire for more ease and joy stemmed from a place of lack. I was desperate for change because things were a struggle. That philosophy I have grown to live by, "be prepared to be surprised", was not always welcomed. Time and time again, the surprises were like a slap in the face. Ideas and dreams that seemed so real quickly felt like a massive waste of time and, even worse, a failure. People I opened my heart to let me down, leaving me feeling alone and disappointed. I learned that it helps to see the circumstances that unfold as chapters of a great novel; you just have not gotten to the good stuff yet. But these chapters are setting you up, preparing you, and even unfolding what is to come. You cannot see it, however. It is easy to say it now, after the fact. But during it, I was a hot mess.

Although it is hard to shake the patterns of negativity, it is possible. I persevered and kept picking myself up. The whole time it felt like failure and struggle. It was also armoring me with strength, skills, and resilience. I am sure that I am not alone in my experience of life in this way. I have met and continue to meet many people who share this universal perspective. I am grateful that I have figured it out. Human nature compels me to share so that someone else may feel more empowered with the things that made the transformation possible for me.

When I learned to look at my patterns and see them deeply, I discovered that I did not feel loved, nor did I love myself. How could I, after all those childhood traumas that left me believing that everyone else's needs were more important than mine and that I was not good enough to be loved?

Thankfully, I figured out how to love myself. It turns out it was kind of basic and yet complicated. Mostly it was a process and took roughly ten years. Ironically that made me feel like a failure. Why was it taking me so long, and why was it so hard for me when all the books and mentors made it seem like it was a simple three-step process? It did happen eventually, but it turned out there were several layers to the topic.

I had to find a level of acceptance and love for myself, which required me to forgive myself, the bad deal I felt I was dealt, and those that hurt me. I had to come to terms with where I came from and what I experienced that left me feeling I was not as good as others. I also discovered that I needed to create a more abundant mindset. An abundant mindset requires a way of thinking that centers on there being enough. I had to train myself to see and believe that there is enough, I have enough, and I am enough. Truthfully this was at the root of my lack of self-love. What a relief I felt when I started to see the world through the eyes of abundance. Wow, I felt so much lighter, and the world felt significantly safer.

It was a welcome change when I transformed my mindset into a more abundant way of thinking and being. The way I saw things changed, my expectations changed, and my behaviors changed. I felt there was enough, so I started acting like there was enough, and now there was more. I was not doing more to get more. I was doing the same, and, in fact, less, yet more was coming to me.

More money, more support, more friendships, more opportunities, and most importantly, more ease and peace of mind. The very thing I craved and was desperate for all my life. The stuff I worked on all those years to have, was now happening. Was it just timing? Or possibly a coincidence? I suppose anything is possible, but there was a distinct change in me and the way I felt. Things were falling into place, and I am grateful, regardless of the explanation.

It is a great feeling. I am loving that I am feeling abundant and loving this person I have discovered I am. Things are feeling good, and my visions of life are manifesting. New opportunities are arising, and I am in awe at the growth I am seeing unfold. I am not perfect, stuff still happens, and I still find myself having fears but thankfully, while it tries to sprout into more and stop me in my tracks, I get a hold of it. I have a regular daily habit of meditation and connecting to my body, which shows me there is something off, and I nip it in the bud.

Life feels safer. I feel lighter and more at ease. I love that feeling; when you have clarity, and you can just let your shoulders relax, it is so refreshing. There is a sense of inner peace and a knowing that overcomes you. I can see the self-love journey I embarked on so many years ago coming full circle - a picture in my head and a knowing in my heart that is difficult to describe in words. I see where I started not loving myself or feeling loved by others. The pattern of failure that played out for so many years was at the root of the lack of love. I bought into this story. I told myself that I was not enough and caused or deserved the challenges I endured. I had the realization that if you do not love yourself, you will never feel worthy of love, and if you do not feel loved by others, you will not feel deserving of love.

Gratitude overflows for the life I now have. It is not because it is perfect. The wish for life to be without issues and never have anything terrible happen is a fairy tale. Learning how to walk through the storm and come out of it is a story of success that will leave you feeling proud.

I have the means to pay witness to my limiting beliefs and even the ability to pluck them out and plant new ways of seeing and being. I can handle struggles with more grace now. I understand that the answers are always in reach. I see that despite how it may appear, it is never as it seems. I know that it is safe to be me. I know that I have lots more life to live. I see that I get to decide how life feels. I know that I have never really failed.

I desire that you, too, come to see and be all of this and more. If you have related to my story and seek to create a more prosperous and peaceful life, I invite you to keep moving forward with an open heart and mind. Start by affirming, "There is enough, I have enough, I am enough, I am safe," and know that you can create the life of health, prosperity, and peace that everyone deserves, including you.

Leanne Giavedoni

"If you have a dream, don't just sit there.
Gather courage to believe that you can succeed and
leave no stone unturned to make it a reality."
— Dr Roopleen

Shannon Levee

GREEN BUTTERFLY

On a Wing and a Prayer

Shannon, "Shan" for short, is an earthy, warm welcoming and shoot the shit kinda girl!

This girl has "Grit" her passion and perseverance despite being confronted by significant obstacles pushed on, overcoming her physical, emotional, and mental health challenges.

Navigating through all her obstacles she managed to raise two beautiful children, the loves of her life, who are also not strangers to adversity. They are a family knit with strength, courage, laughter, and a whole bunch of love.

Shannon shares: " For a long time I didn't love myself enough to go through the pain of change but then I asked for help and embarked on a new love affair with myself"

"Rise to your feet and walk the path to better living with Shannon".

As a Reflexologist, Foot Reader and Healing Coach you are in very good hands with Shan. She starts with your feet, opening the path to your healing. With loving care, she gives you guidance, support, and a shoulder to lean on.

A foot reading with Shannon is not only healing but is supportive and freeing. She shares her inner strength as she travels the journey with you, leading by example.

Shan stays real, regardless of her circumstances, making her a trustworthy ally, the warrior you want on your side when it comes time to face your own battles.

She walks the talk and inspires others to greater achievements through her strong, authentic presence.

Contact information:

- Email: shannonlevee@gmail.com
- Facebook Page: https://www.facebook.com/shannon.smithlevee
- Women's Facebook Group: https://www.facebook.com/groups/yourrustichaven

Linda Foote

A SPECIAL VISIT

When you Ask for a Miracle

"It's your time to enjoy something for yourself and shine. Be the light in your journey!" Linda Foote

In my past life, I was a pre-school and Adjunct Art Teacher and am now a Vision Board Coach and Essential Oil Educator.

I am a graduate of Utica College of Syracuse University. I'm a Certified Yoga Instructor-Evolve Yoga, Reiki 1 Level-Jamie Lee, Animal Bonds, Doterra Essential Oil Specialist, Certified in Meditation from University of Central Florida, Certified Vision Board Coach with Joyce Schrawz

I love life! And yes, I jumped out of an airplane at 60, zip-lined at 62, love swimming in the ocean, and enjoy canoeing with my hubby, Roger. Honestly, there isn't much that I don't like to do. And my husband will tell you that I keep life interesting.

My passion is playing with my Doterra Essential Oils, Creating Art, and living life to the fullest with my awesome hubby of 33 years. Together we are grandparents to eight grandchildren whom we love and cherish beyond, and oh boy, they are keeping us young at heart!

My goal is to guide women struggling with manifesting, discover the power of using essential oils with vision boards and bring their dreams and goals into reality. I will tell you that I don't teach you just to create a cute crafty project. Instead, I guide you on how to prepare first, so you know how to use your vision board, so it works. I am making it my life purpose to share my Creativity and Educate with Kindness to ignite others to Dream with Passion and joy!

I love helping women and showing them they can receive what they want in life. I suffered a mild depression silently after losing my daughter to suicide. My husband, Essential oils, meditating, friends, and a lot of self-development kept me grounded. It's been a long journey, but I now have the right tools to move into the light. Hopefully, my story will help someone who has gone through a rough patch in life. For me, creating vision boards has been therapeutic.

"A Vision Board without a VISION is simply a crafty project."

So, if you are sick of creating crafty vision boards that end up in a drawer, I understand! Because I have been there, I know exactly how you feel! My technique for a POWERFUL vision board is to generate a vision board that reaps the ultimate results.

- You can find me on Facebook, where you can catch my weekly for a Tea chat. So come grab a cup of tea and join me. I love getting to know and meeting new friends. https://www.facebook.com/groups/designyourdreamsgroup
- Website: https://lindasfoote.podia.com

Don't forget to spread kindness throughout your day. Sending hugs!

~

Jennifer Smith Rider

The Labyrinth

A Journey to Wholeness

Jennifer grew up in a small Ontario village, the youngest of five children. Spring saw her planting the gardens alongside

her father and in the fall, she always helped in the preserving
with her mother.

Jennifer is an avid knitter and is a mentor for stroke survivors
and involved in advising provincial strategies for stroke reinte-
gration into the community.

Her dream is to continue to expand her flower garden into a
small flower farm where she can sell her flowers "Buy the
Stem".

She has enjoyed writing and sharing her story and reminds
people to always look forward.

- You can reach out to Jennifer here:
  Smithrider58@gmail.com
- You can find more information regarding strokes here:
  https://www.cdc.gov/stroke/types_of_stroke.htm

Kari Baxter

MY LIFES JOURNEY

Recovering From Drug Addiction

Kari was born in Prince George, in British Columbia, which
sits on the traditional lands of the Lheidli – T'enneh First
Nation, whose name means "people where the rivers come
together" in the Carrier language.

After her birth, her family moved to live with her father's First
Nation Community of Tahltan in a remote area called Tele-
graph Creek. During this time, her mother and father sepa-

rated, and from 10 -15 years of age, Kari was bounced back and forth between her parents, experiencing abuse and living in chaos most of the time.

At 15 years old, Kari moved to Vernon, a small city in the warmth of the Okanagan. It was here that she felt she was able to put down roots.

Kari is the mother of two children, a sweet little boy of five years old and a lovely little girl who is six. Kari realized that she had broken many promises to her children. The love for her children and wanting them to have a better life caused her to dig in and do the work to turn her life around. And that is precisely what this brave young woman did.

Kari has volunteered her time at Vision Quest, an organization that helped her get her life back. She is a resource for other young women struggling with addiction and getting their lives on track.

Kari will never forget the help she received and wants to give back by helping others. Kari works with Lookout Housing and Health Society. Lookout provides housing and a range of support services to adults with low or no income who have few housing or support options.

In her spare time, Kari enjoys date nights with her boyfriend. She loves the outdoors and the mountains and is an avid hiker.

What is most important to Kari is family. Every opportunity she gets to visit, she goes. Her family means the world to her.

You can reach out to Kari at baxterkari.95@gmail.com

If you are curious about how Lookout helps, here is the link.

- https://lookoutsociety.ca/

Michelle Voyageur

UNCONDITIONAL LOVE AND HOW I FOUND IT

How I Built My Family

I am Michelle Voyageur and I live in Prince George, BC. I have lived in this part of BC since I was 12. We moved to a remote place called Cluculz Lake. It's between Prince George and Vanderhoof, but closer to Vanderhoof. We had lived in Ladner, BC before that. My parents had six kids, so life was hectic and hardly ever quiet. I am the second eldest and have four brothers and a sister. I have lived in Prince George since 1983.

I am Chipewyan Cree and was born in Edmonton, AB in 1961. My birth mother surrendered me at birth and left me at the hospital. My foster parents took me in days later and I have remained with my foster mom my entire life. She is simply, mom. I am a mother to three beautiful and strong daughters. They make me so very proud. I am a grandmother of two. My granddaughter is 12 and my grandson is 16. There will also be another granddaughter for me to love and spoil come January 2022!

Being creative was something I have always been. I love writing and through the years, have written stories for my children, poetry for family and friends and now I make greeting cards. It's a passion that fills my days. Who knew I could be so excited to have my own crafting room? It's always been about the arts for me. English class and Art class were where I wanted to be in high school. I've recently taken up painting again. I did have to stop everything though, due to a botched surgery. After four years, I was able to have reconstructive tendon surgery and I have use of my right hand again.

Since being asked to write my chapter in this book series, it is just the beginning for me. I can't count how many people have told me I need to write down my story. There are many aspects to my life, some bad but most have been amazing. My hope is that I can be an inspiration to women. If I can inspire one person to make a change that will better her life, then I'll know I haven't failed.

- My Facebook Business Page: https://www.facebook. com/groups/841240809925166
- My Instagram: https://www.instagram.com/ charliesgirl52/?hl=en

Crystal Marcoux

ADHD & ME

Daily Struggles

Hello, my name is Crystal Marcoux and I was born in Surrey, British Columbia on November, 28th 1984.

I grew in Surrey with my parents and my four older siblings. I currently live with my four beautiful special needs children in Surrey.

I've worked at Surrey Memorial Hospital for the past 16 years as a care aide/patient porter and an educator where I've been able to take my uniqueness of having ADHD and apply it to the care, I give my patients and how I help my coworkers.

I wanted to be a part of this book to help really shed a light on one what it's truly like living with ADHD and the stigmas around it and two what its like being a parent when you have ADHD.

I'm hoping to empower others to embrace their differences and use them to reach your goals because anything is truly possible when you've got the right mind set.

Also, I truly hope this will change people's minds on how they look at and perceive people who are diagnosed with any type of disability.

"It's ok to be me"

Here are a few places people can go to get help with parenting children with challenges.

- https://healthymindslearning.ca - Rolling with ADHD
- https://www.childrens-foundation.org - Cedarwood family program
- https://www2.gov.bc.ca - Child & Youth Mental Health Intake Clinics

~

Ronda Devlin-Gilbert

SHATTERED

Home of the Unwed

Rhonda, High Priestess Lady Rose, I have journeyed on my spiritual path for many decades.

I started my journey seeking my own healing and through ceaseless seeking, study, and initiations I am now, what I like to call myself, a Spiritual Sherpa. And I now have the honor to help guide those who are also seeking healing.

I work with many modalities. As a Mohawk of the Bear Clan Shamanic Healer, a 9th degree Reiki Grandmaster, a Master Tarot Reader, astrologist, medium, Certified Fairyologist (yes that is a thing), artist and more I am blessed to have a large toolbox to pull from. I don't just show you how to navigate the river of life ~ I show you how to pick it up & move it!

But ultimately as your Spiritual Sherpa my job is I get to fall in love with your beautiful Soul and show you how amazing & precious you really are!

Rhonda, Lady Rose, lives in Kingston Ontario, Canada. She's been married to her gorilla and the love of her life for 33 years. Is the proud mother of two. And the proud grandmother of two.

You can find Lady Rose At:

- YouTube ~ Lady Rose of Goddess Garage
  www.YouTube.com/LadyRoseofGoddessGarage
- Join me every Monday evening for Mystic Mondays
  Live at 7pm (Est)
- Facebook at Goddess Garage Tarot Parlour
  www.Facebook.com/thegoddessgarage
- Follow me on Facebook to Book your in person online

Tarot Reading or Healing Soul Session ~ available Worldwide

- Instagram at LadyRoseTarot www.instagram.com/ LadyRoseTarot - Follow me on Instagram to see my Junk Journal Art
- My Etsy Shop is GoddessGarageCanada https:// etsy.me/2VLiC4L

Tammie Trites

THE INVISIBLE DISEASE

Living with Fibromyalgia

Tammie was born and raised in Surrey, British Columbia. She has recently made a move, with her family to Alberta.

Tammie is the mother of five beautiful, amazing daughters and grandmother to three rambunctious grandsons and one sweet little granddaughter. There is never a dull moment in her home. Tammie's home has always been the home for family get togethers and dinners.

Interesting Tammie is an only child, with 10 half brothers and sisters. Tammie's mother and father blended their families and then Tammie was born, the baby of the family. With seven older sisters and three older brothers growing up was not always easy for Tammie.

Tammie wanted to write her story about living with Fibromyalgia in the hopes that those who are experience this disease can gain some insight into what help may be out there for them.

Check this article out if you want to learn more about Fibromyalgia:

https://www.health.harvard.edu/blog/getting-the-best-treatment-for-your-fibromyalgia-2020091020905

~

B'elle Meraki

DRIP LOVE

A Mother's Journey Through Parental Alienation

B'elle Meraki is a pseudonym chosen to protect my child's identity. Though I feel comfortable telling my story, I don't believe it's fair (or a good parenting practice) to tell her story. That's for her to do if she ever feels the need. Having said that, the experience of telling my story in such a public way has been an incredible gift.

The Greek word Meraki means to do something with passion, from the heart, with absolute devotion, with undivided attention, a labor of love. If you knew the real me, you would know that is how I have parented all my children throughout the years. When I set out to tell my story, I did so, intending to tell it in the same spirit I raised my family and hope that someone who had similar experiences would benefit from knowing that they are not crazy and are not alone.

For the most part, I have lived a charmed life. I was raised by great parents who taught me the importance of working in service for others, which led to my calling as a Foster parent for over two dozen children.

I had numerous jobs and careers but Fostering was by far the most fulfilling of all. Beyond the opportunity to open my home and heart for children at a time when they needed it, I also was able to advocate for families and children who were struggling with the child welfare system.

I have been blessed with three daughters, two grandchildren, and the best third husband ever!

Our love story began when we were six years old, and after a 40 + year break, we were reunited on my 50th Birthday. His love and support were instrumental in my survival of Parental Alienation, and I will be forever grateful that he was brought back into my life when he was.

If you would like to reach out, please contact me at bellemeraki3@gmail.com

Sheri Godfrey

PITY PARTY OR CHAMPAGNE?

When Death knocks on your door, how will you answer?

Born and raised in Nova Scotia, Sheri's foundational values have always been based on helping your neighbor. We grew up just adding another chair to the table in a time of need – especially for those challenging times and tough conversations.

When my mom was diagnosed with Ovarian Cancer, it opened my eyes to how I viewed End of Life and our Time on Earth. After some investigating, I was called to become a Certified

End of Life Doula. For me, helping a loved one – mine or yours- navigate the last chapter of life is a very rewarding honor. My path has twisted and turned, and I am honored to help families navigate transitions.

I enjoy being active with my husband Tim in my downtown and enjoy sleepovers with my Grandson Jaxon as he keeps me young at heart.

I am Certified as an End Of Life Doula through Douglas College, and I am here to have those difficult conversations with you and your family.

I understand the challenges and the emotions. My mother's aggressive in-curable Ovarian Cancer diagnosis prompted me to become certified to help other families navigate these challenging times.

Death is a guarantee for each of us. When we can make these conversations part of our everyday vocabulary, families can move through final days with greater understanding, love, compassion, and support.

Don't leave your End of Life plan to the bitter end – pre-planning really does lift a weight off of your shoulders, and it does create ease and grace for your family.

If you would like to get more information or speak with me, reach out to one of the links below.

- Website: www.seniortransitions.solutions
- Website: www.sherigodfeyy.ca
- Linkedin: https://www.linkedin.com/in/sheri-godfrey-160421111/
- Email: sheri@seniortransitions.solutions

∼

Leanne Giavedoni

FROM SCARCITY TO SIMPLY SPLENDID

A story of transforming struggle to manifest a life of abundance and grace.

During her long career as a physiotherapist, wellness coach and educator, Leanne Giavedoni found herself increasingly fascinated with how to overcome struggles, find healing and experience success. Leanne has dedicated over two decades to coaching people to connect within so that they can create better emotional and physical well-being.

Leanne Giavedoni is the author of "Fear Unravelled" and founder of Unleashed Essentials. At Unleashed Essentials we share an integrative model of health & wellness that bridges traditional with alternative approaches. We help you create better health, prosperity, and peace using a mind-body-spirit approach that bridges the gap that is apparent in traditional approaches to health & wellness.

When she isn't sharing her passion, you will find Leanne communing with nature, planning her next travel excursion or relaxing with her high-school sweetheart, son, and daughter in their rural home near Hamilton, Ontario.

Learn more about at:

- Website: www.leannegiavedoni.com
- Reach me here: essentials@leannegiavedoni.com
- Join my Facebook Group: https://www.facebook.com/groups/fearunravelled/

I'm Julie Fairhurst. Author, Speaker, Sales, and Marketing Specialist. Founder of Women Like Me – an Amazon Number One Best Selling Series and Rock Star Publishing.

I grew up in an abusive home where poverty and alcoholism were ramped. I knew I didn't want to live this way. But how do you change what you've always known?

Single mom for 24 years, living off government handouts, standing in line at food banks to feed my kids. At Christmas, I received food hampers and presents for my kids from charities. Not an easy path to change, but I did it!

Now, I have over 30 years of business experience in marketing, promotion, and sales. An award-winning professional, I am using my expertise to help female entrepreneurs and women struggling with the promotion of themselves through their stories.

I understand the courage, resilience, and perseverance to tell your story to the world because I am a woman like you.

I help women heal by telling their stories, releasing themselves from their past. Through the book program Women Like Me, women write their personal stories sharing them to help others and promote healing in the world.

Storytelling helps you be a better communicator. You gain an emotional connection with your audience. Telling your story will spark a connection with them and draw your audience to you.

In the Women Like Me Academy, I will guide you through the writing process and becoming a Published Author for entrepreneurs. You will receive promotion, marketing, and sales training so you can take your story out into the world and use it for your speaking, coaching, or writing career.

For more information: www.womenlikemeacadmey.com

You know, some people would say never to look back, but I do every day. Why? Because I never want to forget the journey that led me to where I am today. And today, my life is entirely different. I didn't just fall into this new life. I worked at it every day, all the time.

Wishing for you that you can live your best life, the life you came here to live.

Julie Fairhurst

Want to reach out? There are many ways to find me.

Email: julie@changeyourpath.ca

Join the Movement on Facebook:

Come to the community and spent time with other inspiring women. We are waiting for you!

Women Like Me Community – Julie Fairhurst

https://www.facebook.com/groups/879482909307802

Rock Star Strategies

www.rockstarstrategies.com

Women Like Me Stories

www.womenlikemestories.com

Follow Women Like Me Stories Blog

https://womenlikemestories.com/category/blog/

Find me on Social Media:

Rock Star Strategies on Facebook

https://www.facebook.com/juliefairhurstcoaching

LinkedIn

https://www.linkedin.com/in/womenlikemestories/

Instagram

https://www.instagram.com/womenlikemestories/

If you want to buy books, there are two ways to do that.

Women Like Me Books

https://womenlikemestories.com/buy-books/

Amazon – search Julie Fairhurst in the search bar or go here...

https://www.amazon.com/s?k=julie+fairhurst&ref=nb_sb_noss

Amazon Author Page – if you click on any of my books, the profile is there, or go here...

https://www.amazon.com/s?k=julie+fairhurst&ref=nb_sb_noss

Other Books by Julie Fairhurst

Women Like Me Series

- Women Like Me – A Celebration of Courage and Triumphs
- Women Like Me – Stories of Resilience and Courage
- Women Like Me – A Tribute to the Brave and Wise
- Women Like Me – Breaking Through the Silence
- Positivity Makes all the Difference

Mindset

- Your Mindset Matters
- Build Your Self-Esteem – 100 Tips designed to boost your confidence
- Self-Esteem Journal

Sales Books

- Agent Etiquette – 14 Things You Didn't Learn in Real Estate School
- 7 Keys to Success – How to Become a Real Estate Sales Badass
- Net Marketing
- 30 Days To Real Estate Action
- 100 Reasons Agents Quit The Business

Acknowledgments

A special thank you to all my co-authors of Women Like me – Breaking Through the Silence. It has been an honor to work with you, eleven outstanding women. You are all quite remarkable, and I am blessed to know every one of you.

Breaking Through the Silence became the subtitle for volume four once your stories began to be told. You all have broken through the silence in very different ways.

For some of you, it was removing the shame of disabilities and shining your light on how others could reach out for help for.

More of you opened up about past traumas that most of us would never have been able to do. You opened your hearts and release you story to the world. You brave ladies did it. And you will help so many with your courage.

Some of you broke free from addictions, one of the hardest things to do, but you did it. And because of you, others experiencing similar situations in their lives will move forward towards a healthier life.

And others wrote about standing up for yourself and others in the world. As women, we have been taught to "keep quiet" and not speak our minds. This could have been past down from our previous generations. You ladies knew it was time to stand up and use your voice. Other women will be able to find their voices because of your examples.

I celebrate all of you for your growth during the process of writing your stories for Women Like Me. It is a complicated process, especially when you have not written before. But you did it, ladies, and this is a beautiful book full of inspiration and love because of you all.

I'm so very proud of you all.

Your friend Julie

∿

To you, the reader

I appreciate your support. It means everything to the authors and, of course, to me.

It is a daunting task to write about your personal life, especially when there is trauma, illness, and inner work that the writers are describing. It is vulnerable to put themselves out there and share their personal lives with the world.

I can honestly tell you, each of the women who wrote their story in Women Like Me does it because they understand that others are in need, and they hope through telling their story, that other women will read their story and decide for themselves to live their best lives. Every writer asks me, "do you think my story will help others." And I tell them YES!

Of course, they write for other personal reasons, but knowing that they can help another by telling their story to heal their life is at the forefront of their minds as they write.

If you felt a women's story in the book helped you along your path in life, you can go and leave a message. I will be sure to pass it along to the author. It would be my pleasure to do that for you.

www.womenlikemestories.com

Special Thank You... once again

Jennifer Sparks – Stoke Publishing

Jen is someone you want in your corner if you're writing a book or learning how to be self-published. Her knowledge is outstanding in the publishing arena. Jen was always there for any questions I had and was a guide for getting Women Like Me published.

I am incredibly grateful to have been able to work with Jen and look forward to working with her on more publishing projects.

If you would like to reach out to Jennifer, visit:

- jennysparks@hotmail.ca
- www.stokepublishing.com

- www.instagram.com/stokepub/

Christine Luciani - More than just a Virtual Assistant

Thank you again, Christine, for all your support and hard work with this book and everything else I do! You are appreciated and loved. It's wonderful to know you are there and on my side. Thank you for being there, yet once again.

Rob Breaks – My partner in life

You continue to support me with love and belief. You are always ready to listen and give me the feedback I need, believing in me and all my wild ideas. Never once complaining that you "again" had to prepare our dinner as I was on zoom calls with writers or in the middle of a book launch.

You treat everything I do as important, and I love you for that. Thanks for being my rock.

Would you like to be an author in the book series?

Women Like Me?

Do you have a story that needs to be told? A story that may be holding you back from living your best life? Or possibly, you have overcome and are ready to share with the world, hoping that your story will invoke another to live a better life?

Writing is therapeutic to the soul. Writing about your past events can be beneficial, both emotionally and physically. You can increase your feelings of well-being and even enhance your immune system.

We only get one chance. Our lives are not a dress rehearsal for our next lifetime. We only get this one life, and it's here, and it's now.

Reach out to me at www.womelikemestories.com and let me know you are ready to tell your story. The world is waiting for you.

Women Like Me Academy

FOR WOMEN IN BUSINESS

There is massive power in stories! And, in your story!

Have you ever noticed that many celebrities repeat parts of their stories in almost every interview they do? That's because there is immense power in our stories. But it needs to be the right story that will align with your business.

In the academy, we will flush out your story. Once you've written your chapter in the book, we will move to promote you and your story to the world.

Your prospective clients will be drawn to you because you will connect to them through your story. You will leave the academy with promotional pieces that you can use to promote your story, your business, and you personally.

If you would like to learn more about the academy, you can reach me at julie@changeyourpath.ca.